BEHOLD YOUR GOD

DONALD MACLEOD

CHRISTIAN FOCUS PUBLICATIONS

'It is impossible to honour God as we ought,
unless we know Him as He is.'

Stephen Charnock

Published by
CHRISTIAN FOCUS PUBLICATIONS LTD

ISBN 1 871676 50 9

Contents

PREFACE

It is probably not the function of a preface to pre-empt criticism but in this particular case the attempt may be forgiven. The various chapters which follow are unequal in length and uneven in level; the treatment of the topic is far from exhaustive; and the allusions to the relevant literature are patchy.

All of which may amount to a very good argument against the book appearing at all. But the publishers did ask for it; and there is a real dearth in English of biblically-oriented books on the attributes of God. The very real defects referred to above reflect the fact that most of these chapters have already been published in some form elsewhere; that they began life as lectures or addresses; and that the audiences to which they were originally delivered varied widely.

The basic outlook behind the book is indicated in the Introduction, but this is slightly more technical than the remaining chapters and the busy reader may skip it. In sum, it indicates that I write from the stand-point of Protestant orthodoxy, but very much regret the way that the spirit of Scholasticism clung to discussions of the doctrine of God long after it was banished from other areas of theology. Over against this I have tried to reflect the specifically biblical approach to the divine attributes; and also to do justice to the fact the Christ is the supreme revelation of God. If the book has one master-idea it is the sentiment once expressed by the late Archbishop Michael Ramsey: 'God is Christ-like and in Him there is no un-Christlikeness at all' (*God, Christ and the World,* SCM Press, London, 1969, p. 98). But while I have the utmost admiration for academics this book is not aimed at them. It is aimed at the kind of intelligent lay-people who originally requested the talks from which the book was born.

With such a flimsy product it may seem pretentious to thank those who helped. But various people did make valuable suggestions, many of which I adopted. In particular, I should like to thank Dr Donald MacKenzie of the Department of English Literature at Glasgow University; Professor Sinclair Ferguson of Westminster Theological Seminary, Philadelphia, USA; and the Rev. A.T.B. McGowan of Trinity Possil and Henry Drummond Church of Scotland, Glasgow.

Thanks are also due to the staff of Christian Focus Publications, not least for their patience and perseverance.

Finally, a note on the biblical quotations. These follow no particular version. Most of them reflect my personal understanding of the original texts; and in a few instances I have paraphrased, to strengthen a particular emphasis.

Donald Macleod

Edinburgh, November, 1989.

INTRODUCTION

The doctrine of God has naturally been an object of intensive study throughout the history of the Christian church. The results of that study are conveniently available in standard theological textbooks such as Hodge's *Systematic Theology*, Shedd's *Dogmatic Theology* and Berkhof's *Systematic Theology*. They are also encapsulated in many more comprehensive studies. Charnock's *Discourses on the Existence and Attributes of God* (r.i. Grand Rapids, 1979) and Kaiser's *The Doctrine of God* (London, 1982) come most readily to mind. Behind these, in turn, lies the painstaking thoroughness of the seventeenth century dogmaticians. These are the so-called Protestant Scholastics whose work is brilliantly summarised in Heppe's *Reformed Dogmatics* (r.i. Grand Rapids, 1978, pp. 57-104) and who, themselves, were drawing on the mediaeval theologians, particularly Anselm and Aquinas.

There is much that is excellent in this legacy. But twentieth century theologians, from Barth downwards, have expressed serious misgivings not only about the detailed conclusions of traditional study but about the whole framework within which it has been set. Barth was particularly critical of the practice of beginning the study of theology with a doctrine of God *in general* (one on which all men could agree, on the assumption that it was *natural* rather than *revealed*): 'The result was an involuntary movement away from the school of Scripture into that of heathen antiquity. The nature of God was defined as a neuter furnished with every conceivable superlative, as the *ENS PERFECTISSIMUM* and the *SUMMUM BONUM*, which as such, as the *ACTUS PURUS* of the spirit is also the *PRIMUM MOVENS*' (*Church Dogmatics, Vol. II, Pt. I, p. 288*).

Emil Brunner, characteristically, expressed himself more forcefully, arguing that in their doctrine of the divine attributes the Protestant scholastic theologians reverted entirely to the mediaeval metaphysic: 'The theological doctrine of the Divine Attributes handed on from the theology of the Early Church has been shaped by the Platonic and Neo-Platonic Idea of God, and not by the biblical data ... Anyone who comes for the first time from the Bible into the world of Scholastic Theology feels himself in a foreign world' (*The Christian Doctrine of God, London, 1949, p. 243 f.*).

Barth and Brunner, of course, represent a particular theological school and one which itself sometimes showed scant respect for Scripture (witness Brunner's view of the Virgin Birth: *The Mediator,* London, 1936, p.322 ff.) But other scholars have shared their disquiet over the historical development of the doctrine of God. John Calvin, for example, spoke of the philosophers' 'stupidity and want of sense', deprecated the 'vain, indolent, slumbering omnipotence which sophists (i.e. scholastics) feign' and pointed out that 'there was no pure and authentic religion founded merely on common belief' (*Institutes* I:V, 11; I:XVI,3;I:V,13). Charles Hodge, too, was conscious of the problem (*Systematic Theology,* Vol. I, p. 394): 'It is deeply to be regretted that not only the Fathers, but also the Lutheran and Reformed theologians, after renouncing the authority of the schoolmen, almost immediately yielded themselves to their speculations. Instead of determining the nature of the divine attributes from the representations of Scripture and from the constitution of man as the image of God, and from the necessities of our moral and religious nature, they allowed themselves to be controlled by *a priori* speculations as to the nature of the infinite and absolute'. (Unfortunately, Hodge himself was not all that successful in trying to shake off the scholastic influence.) William Cunningham was even more severe, noting that the main feature of Scholasticism was its reliance on Aristotelian dialectics, lamenting the almost total absence of strictly theological method (exegesis) and concluding that scholastic theology consisted mainly of 'the discussion of useless and unprofitable questions, which cannot be determined, and which would be of no practical value if they could' (*Historical Theology,* Vol. I, p. 413 ff.).

These criticisms vary in matters of detail, but there is one obvious common factor: the traditional doctrine is too far removed from the thought-world of the Bible and too much influenced by philosophy. So far as particular influences are concerned, the main culprits have been Platonism, Neo-Platonism and Aristotelianism. These determined the questions and shaped the answers of Scholastic theology and Reformed dogmatics accepted this agenda almost unquestioningly.

Anyone trying to assess this situation must proceed with caution. As G.L. Prestige points out (*God in Patristic Thought,* London, 1952, p. xxiii), 'There are always dangers in thinking', and the only way to avoid making problematical statements about God is to avoid thinking and speaking of Him altogether. Besides, the aversion to Scholasticism often reflects an aversion to theology as such; and the plea for a reverent agnosticism may be no more than an irreverent rejection of biblical revelation. Scripture provides more material for propositional theology than many modern scholars are prepared to admit. The scholastics may sometimes have given the impression that they knew what God has for breakfast, but at least they felt confident that God had shared with man a significant amount of what He knows about Himself.

In fact, many of the alleged blemishes of mediaeval theology did not originate with Scholasticism at all. They are already prominent in the writings of the earliest Christian Fathers. The evidence for this is conveniently available in Prestige's work already cited. These early theologians had no compunction, for example, about indulging in fanciful speculation as to the original meaning of the term *god*. Nor did they avoid abstract terms. They refer to God repeatedly as the Good, the Ingenerate, the First Principle. They also made free use of negative expressions: God is indivisible, invisible, intangible and incomposite. He is without beginning. He is not contained in space. He is uncreated. He is incomprehensible.

Above all, it was the Fathers, not the Scholastics, who introduced the idea of the impassibility of God: 'It is invariably assumed and repeatedly stated that impassibility is one of the divine attributes' (Prestige, *op. cit.*, p. 6.). Gregory of Nazianzus, for example, spoke of Christ as 'passible in His flesh, impassible in His godhead' (*Letter to Cledonius Against Apollinaris* [*Epistle 101*]). Athanasius expresses similar sentiments: 'While He Himself was in no way injured, being impassible and incorruptible and very word of God, He maintained and preserved in His own impassibility men who were suffering' (*On the Incarnation of the Word,* 54). Nor was this some late development. Some of the very earliest Fathers spoke in exactly the same way. Ignatius' *Epistle to Polycarp* was written in the early years of the second century and already we find the idea of impassibility taken for granted: 'Anoint Him that is above every season, the Eternal, the Invisible, who became visible for our sake, the Impalpable, the Impassible, who suffered for our sake' (*To Saint Polycarp, 3*).

These are the three details for which scholastic theology has been most severely castigated: its speculative tendencies, its use of negative concepts and its *a priori* assumption that God cannot suffer. But these were not scholastic innovations at all. They are already prominent in the theology of the early Fathers.

In fact, one can go even further. Some of the distinctive procedures of scholastic dogmatics are clearly to be found in the Scriptures themselves. This is particularly true of *the three ways* by which, according to mediaeval theology, we could attain to the knowledge of God: the way of negation, the way of eminence and the way of causality. The Bible does not, of course, formally endorse these, but it contains clear evidence of all three procedures.

In the way of negation, all imperfection is denied to God. This is a frequent occurrence in Scripture. We find it, for instance, in the great description of God in Isaiah 40:28. He does not faint or become weary. His understanding is unsearchable. In Deuteronomy 4:12, the Lord reminds Israel that when He spoke to them they saw no similitude. In Malachi 3:6, He insists, 'I the Lord do not change'. And according to 1 Timothy 1:17, He is immortal and invisible. The way of negation clearly has the sanction of Scripture.

The same is true of the way of eminence, according to which human qualities are ascribed to God but in an exalted degree. There is a clear example of it in Isaiah 49:15: 'Can a woman forget her sucking child, that she should have no compassion on the son of her womb? Even these may forget, but I will not forget you.' It occurs, too, in Psalm 103: 13: 'As a father pities his children, so the Lord pities those who fear him'. Human virtues and excellencies are but pale shadows of the glory of the Almighty.

Equally clearly, the Bible endorses the way of causality: what God is can be deduced from what God does. This appears in the passage from Isaiah already quoted: it is precisely because He is the Creator of the ends of the earth that God cannot be thought to be weary or ignorant (Isaiah 40:28). In the same way the psalmist's sense of security rests on the fact that his Lord made heaven and earth (Psalm 121:2). The way of causality is also the basis of the appeal in Psalm 94:9: 'He who planted the ear, does he not hear? He who formed the eye, does he not see?' The Lord Himself uses a similar argument in Matthew 6:26,30. God's commitment to His children can be inferred from the fact that He clothes the lilies and feeds the birds.

Clearly, then, unthinking criticism of scholastic theology can very quickly betray us into criticism of the whole approach of Scripture itself. But even when it comes to the charge, 'Too philosophical!' the case against Scholasticism is by no means clear-cut. The mere presence of philosophical influence cannot itself be a fatal objection to any theological statement. In fact, as James McCosh pointed out in his Introduction to the 1864 edition of *The Works of Stephen Charnock* (Vol. I, pp. xxxvi, xlviii) 'Christian theology cannot be constructed without philosophical principles. ...It will be difficult for the theologian, difficult even for the preacher, to avoid proceeding on an implied philosophy'.

There are four reasons for this.

First, all theology, and indeed all human discourse, proceeds on certain assumptions; and these inevitably have a philosophical colouring. The Bible itself, for example, assumes (and never formally proves) the existence of God. Theologians such as Chalmers and Hodge assumed the maxims of the Common Sense School of Scottish Philosophy. Modern theology generally assumes the epistemology of Immanuel Kant and particular varieties of it are heavily indebted to Heidegger, Wittgenstein and Whitehead. All of us assume our own existence, the reliability of our senses (for example in reading the Scriptures) and the law of contradiction. Even those who protest most loudly against philosophy have to operate with a basic metaphysic.

Secondly, each age must express the faith in terms of its own concepts. The New Testament itself did this, using such words as *form, image, effulgence and likeness* to express Christ's relation to God. Later generations expressed the same truth by means of *nature, substance* and *person.* It was the same in other departments. In defining the Christian doctrine of the atonement theologians drew heavily on jurisprudence. More recently, they have begun to use the concepts of sociology. There is no reason to ban such an approach when dealing with the doctrine of God. The great biblical idea of the divine fatherhood, for example, is surely brilliantly illuminated by the legal concept of adoption. The practice becomes reprehensible only when we forget the provisional and transitional character of all philosophical systems and begin to twist and bend our theology to force it into our preconceived moulds. It has happened too often that concepts introduced as illustrations have quickly become first-principles.

Thirdly, theology always requires arrangement; and whatever method we use, it will imply philosophical principles relating to priorities, analysis and modes of argument. From this point of view there is nothing reprehensible in the Scholastics' use of Aristotle's distinctions between material cause, efficient cause, formal cause and final cause. We ourselves are being equally philosophical when we distinguish between definitive and progressive sanctification or between individual and general eschatology; or when our monographs adopt a historical approach, beginning with the Old Testament, moving through the successive layers of the New Testament and then surveying the history of post-biblical thought before giving a statement of our conclusions. The arrangement may not be Aristotelian but it is certainly dialectical.

Fourthly, to some degree at least theology must engage the questions posed by philosophy. This is partly because philosophy wants to pose objections and we cannot ignore them. But it is partly also because theological (that is, biblical) material itself gives rise to philosophical questions such as the relation of God to time and space, the relation of divine sovereignty to human freedom and the relation of foreordination to causation. Furthermore, philosophy (not always unhelpfully) asks theology to clarify its language and concepts. What do we mean by *person*, by *omnipotence*, by *omnipresence*, by *holiness* ? Honest attempts at clarification will inevitably give philosophical colouring to our theology. But this is hardly fatal.

And yet it is difficult to disagree with Brunner: anyone who moves for the first time from the Bible into the world of scholastic theology does indeed find himself in an alien environment. A cursory perusal of the chapter on the Attributes of God in Heppe's *Reformed Dogmatics* is sufficient to establish this. Here is a typical example: 'Like all attributes of the absolute nature, His will also is essentially a single actuosity eternally identical with itself, which appears like a manifold of various indications and effects only in relation to the manifold of objects. As God knows everything by one intuition and single act of thinking, so also He wills and has willed by one act of will, i.e. by a single volition, Himself and all things present, past, future, necessary, contingent, absolute and conditioned, good and bad, from eternity, by a most free and absolute will' (p. 82).

Whether this is true or false (it is probably true) it is not the language of the Bible nor the language of evangelism nor the language of prayer. To a lesser extent the same charge can be laid against Charnock and Bavinck.

But is it possible to be more specific? What exactly has gone wrong?

The first problem is the linguistic register in which the doctrine of God has been set forth. It is largely non-biblical and highly Latinate: simplicity, aseity, immensity, unity, immutability, infinity, omnipotence, omniscience, omnipresence, justice. The problem is not merely that these words, all derived from Latin, are not found in Scripture. What the language in fact betrays is that the discussion took place in the schools, for scholars: not in the church, for the people of God. Furthermore, it was divorced from biblical control. It was not an exposition of biblical concepts or a quest for biblical definitions.

Nor did the discussion reflect biblical proportion and balance. Calvin (*Institutes* I. X, 2) spoke of the attributes 'it is necessary to know' as lovingkindness, judgment and righteousness. But these were certainly not the most prominent points in traditional dogmatics. Mediaeval theologians were beguiled, instead, by subtle questions relating to the divine simplicity, power, knowledge and will. These were the subject of endless debate and hair-splitting distinctions (for example, between necessary knowledge, free knowledge and middle knowledge; or between *VOLUNTAS BENEPLACITI* and *VOLUNTAS SIGNI*; and *VOLUNTAS DECERNENS* and *VOLUNTAS PRAECIPIENS*). The problem here is not the answers, but the questions. Scripture has no interest in them. They belong to a thought-world light-years away from the Bible.

By contrast, some of the most prominent biblical concepts scarcely appear at all in scholastic dogmatics. One would never guess, reading Heppe, that the New Testament tells us that 'God is love' (1 John 4:8). Brunner is absolutely correct when he points out that 'the doctrine of the love of God was terribly meagre among the Protestant scholastic theologians' (*op. cit.*, p. 203). Sadly, later Reformed dogmatics failed to make good this deficiency. The Shorter Catechism does not mention *love* in its list of divine attributes (Answer 4) and there is no chapter on it in either Charnock or Bavinck. All of these are content to subsume the divine love under the divine goodness. This does no justice whatever to the New Testament's emphasis. There, love is the supreme message of Calvary (itself the supreme word about God), the source of our election and the very essence of God's nature. In this area, traditional dogmatics has been guilty of heresy by disproportion.

But even when attention was focused on specifically biblical attributes the definitions offered were often far from biblical. Mastricht, for example, defined God's love as 'the essential property or essence of God, whereby delighting Himself in it He wishes it the good which He approves' (Heppe, *op. cit.*, p.

95). Maybe. But is this really the message of John 3:16? The problem is even more serious with regard to the divine righteousness. Calvin caught the predominant biblical meaning perfectly: The divine righteousness is that 'by which the faithful are preserved and most benignantly cherished' (*Institutes*, I. X, 2). But later theologians did not remain faithful to this insight. Probably misled by the Vulgate's *IUSTITIA* they focused on justice and retribution rather than on the fact that God's rectitude in covenant-keeping would lead Him to save and vindicate His people. The result can be seen clearly in, for example, Shedd's *Dogmatic Theology* (Vol. I, p. 364 ff.). Shedd consistently speaks of justice rather than righteousness, subsumes it under holiness and concentrates throughout on the element of retribution. Herman Bavinck, however, was aware of the difficulty. While the primary (etymological) meaning seems to be the forensic, in Scripture the element of remuneration is much more prominent than the element of retribution: 'God's righteousness is usually taken 'in a favourable sense' and described as that attribute by virtue of which God justifies the righteous, and exalts them to glory and honour' (*The Doctrine of God*, p. 217).

Something similar happened to the concepts of God's power and presence. Theology lost sight of the redemptive edge of these terms as used in biblical revelation. In fact, there are few sadder aspects to this subject than the radical disjunction between the *religious* idea of the divine presence and the *theological* idea of His omnipresence. The Bible is full of rich allusions to the presence of God and the same is true of the devotional literature of Christianity. But dogmatics ignored this almost completely and focused instead on an impersonal concept of omnipresence, seen as an aspect of the divine immensity and defined as meaning that 'God is a sphere or circle whose centre is everywhere and circumference nowhere' (cited as 'a good expression' by Charnock, *op. cit.*, Vol I, p. 367). The alienation between dogmatics and devotion could not have been more complete.

But it was also seen in discussions of the divine power. In Scripture, this attribute is related in the closest possible way to redemption. God shows His power in the cross, in the resurrection, in the new birth and in the preservation of His people. Later discussion became enmeshed in much more abstruse questions as to the nature of the possible, the distinction between absolute and ordained power and the relation between what God *does* do and what God *could* do. Is God's omnipotence exhausted in the actual occurrences of history? Such questions, if Milton is to be believed, are matters of keen interest to the demons in Pandemonium, who

'reasoned high
Of Providence, Foreknowledge, Will and Fate —
Fixed fate, free will, foreknowledge absolute —
And found no end, in wandering mazes lost'
(*Paradise Lost* II. 558 ff.)

But they are hardly pressing concerns to those facing the urgencies of the Christian life: 'For me, to live is Christ' (Philippians 1: 21).

Too often, too, philosophical preconceptions have kept the church from hearing what God is actually saying about Himself in Scripture. This has been particularly true of the dogma of the impassibility of God: what the Greek Fathers called His *APATHEIA*. Men began with the assumption of the absoluteness and immutability of God and went on to lay down the principle that He was passionless and incapable of suffering. John of Damascus, for example, simply assumed that God was 'without flux and passionless' as surely as He was unchangeable and unalterable (*Exposition of the Orthodox Faith*, I.viii). This was particularly important in connection with the generation of the Son: 'In God, who alone is passionless and unalterable and immutable and ever so continueth, both begetting and creating are passionless' (*loc. cit.*). Clement of Alexandria put it even more strongly: 'God is impassible, free of anger, destitute of desire' (*The Stromata,* IV.xxiii).

As we have seen, this was no late development. It appears already, full-grown, in Ignatius. But it is not absolutely clear what such statements were meant to convey. There is some evidence that what the Fathers were denying was not that God had emotions but that He lacked self-control. Prestige (*op, cit.*, p. 6) argues that, to the Fathers, impassibility represented God's transcendence and moral freedom. He was 'incapable of being diverted or overborne by forces or passions such as commonly hold sway in the creation and among mankind'. This may be so. But some of the Fathers' statements are very strong. Clement, for example, not only warns against 'interpreting the will of the impassible Deity similarly to our own perturbations' but does so in an attempt to refute the idea that God can know either joy or sorrow (*The Stromata*, II.xxvi).

The lengths to which later writers went in asserting the impassibility of God can be seen in Stephen Charnock. The great Puritan, whose *Discourses* are in many respects invaluable, will not allow his God to be touched by repentance, anger, joy or grief: 'Because He is said to have anger and repentance we must not conclude Him to have passions like us ... Grief is not in God ... We may understand those expressions of joy, and grief, and repentance to signify this much, that the things declared to be the objects of joy and grief and repentance are of that nature that *if God were capable of our passions* He would discover Himself in such cases as we do' (*op. cit.*, p. 401 f., italics mine).

The twentieth century has witnessed a strong reaction against such teaching. The strongest reaction, undoubtedly, has come from Jurgen Moltmann, particularly in his book *The Crucified God* (SCM Press, London, 1974): 'Were God incapable of suffering in any respect, and therefore in an absolute sense, then He would also be incapable of love' (*op. cit.*, p. 230). Moltmann approaches the problem specifically from the standpoint of the cross, arguing that here the grief of the Father is just as important as the death of the Son: 'The Son suffers dying, the Father suffers the death of the Son. The Fatherlessness of the Son is matched by the Sonlessness of the Father' (*op. cit.*, p. 243).

But Moltmann's has not been the only voice. Nor was it the first one. Karl Barth had already spoken plainly: 'The personal God has a heart. He can feel and be affected. He is not impassible. He cannot be moved from outside by an extraneous power. But this does not mean that He is not capable of moving Himself' (*Church Dogmatics*, II. I, p. 370). Among British theologians, Oliver Quick questioned the traditional doctrine of divine impassibility because of its implications for the incarnation (*Doctrines of the Creed*, London, 1938, pp. 122-7, 184-7). More recently James Packer has added his voice: 'The divine changelessness of which Scripture speaks must be understood not as an eternally frozen pose, but as the Creator's moral constancy and consistency' (*God Who is Rich in Mercy* : Essays presented to Dr DB Knox, edited by PT O'Brien and DG Petersen, Lancer Books, New South Wales, 1986, p. 16). In the light of this, according to Dr Packer, we need to re-think the doctrine of God's impassibility. It cannot mean impassivity, unconcern and detachment in face of the creation; nor insensitivity and indifference to the distresses of a fallen world; nor inability and unwillingness to empathise with human pain and grief: 'but simply that God's experiences do not come upon Him as ours come upon us, for His are foreknown, willed and chosen by Himself, and are not involuntary surprises forced on Him from outside' *(op. cit.*, p. 17).

Voices have also been raised in support of the traditional doctrine, however. GC Berkouwer repeatedly raises the issue of *THEOPASCHITISM* in his study *The Work of Christ* (Grand Rapids, 1965, pp. 18, 61, 265, 280), concluding that 'the theopaschitic tendency in the new doctrine of reconciliation is a human attempt to present the trinitarian background of the incarnation in a logical synthesis. But in so doing it oversteps the limits of speculation'. The philosophical and hermeneutical assumptions underlying the denial of impassibility have been challenged by Bruce Ware in a significant article in the *Westminster Theological Journal* (Vol. XLVIII, No. 2).

This discussion is far from over. But already it has highlighted two issues. First, the need for biblical control of our doctrine of God. The word *APATHEIA* does not occur in Scripture. If it is to remain in theological use we need to be careful that the idea it represents does not lead to distortion and suppression of biblical truth. This is the primary concern of such scholars as James Packer: we need to treat 'the revelational status' of statements which refer to grief and repentance on the part of God as seriously as we do other biblical statements. Such language is indeed anthropomorphic. But then, the entire biblical representation of God is anthropomorphic (and validly so, because we are made in God's image) and those particular anthropomorphisms tell us as much about God's intention and attributes as do any others. In particular, they emphasise the personalness of God and the warmth of that personalness. The danger of all attempts to speak of God in *pure* language (that is, in language *purer* than Scripture) is that we may reduce Him to an inert, immobile, abstraction: the *ENS PURISSIMUM*. From this point of view, John AT Robinson's *Honest to God* is, paradoxically, the logical terminus of Scholastic theology. The Living God has become the Ground of Being.

Secondly, the debate about impassibility has emphasised the need for *Christological* control of our doctrine of God. What could be more obvious: Christ is the word of God; He is His form, image and glory; to see Him is to see the Father? Sadly, all this was largely forgotten. Yet surely this was the greatest single fact about the Christian revelation of God: 'I decided to know nothing among you except Jesus Christ and him crucified' (1 Corinthians 2:2). The cross, said Luther, is the test of everything (*CRUX PROBAT OMNIA*).

In the light of such considerations, what are we to say of the idea that God is passionless and incapable of suffering?

There are some aspects of the traditional doctrine which we can accept unhesitatingly. For example, God could not suffer physically because He has no body. Nor could God suffer any internal emotional disturbance or upheaval of the kind we experience as a result of unresolved mental conflicts and imperfect integration of our personalities. He cannot lose His composure or show symptoms of stress and agitation. Further, there cannot be in God any merely passive suffering — suffering of which He is only the victim without being also its Foreordainer and Controller. Suffering cannot 'come at' Him — or, to use James' phrase, He cannot simply 'fall in with' it (James 1:2. The same word is used in Luke 10:30 of the man who 'fell among' robbers while on the way to Jericho.). He can only experience it if He takes it and goes towards it. For God, suffering can only be a form of action.

But serious questions remain.

First, the idea that God is a passionless, emotionally immobile Being is totally unscriptural. The Bible reveals Him as a God of wrath and jealousy. It also reveals Him as One who has no pleasure in the death of the wicked (Ezekiel 33:11) and therefore, by implication, as One who is grieved when human beings destroy themselves. The New Testament even describes the Holy Spirit specifically as capable of grief (Ephesians 4:30). Similarly, God is revealed as One who is passionate in His love, loving the church as a husband loves his wife, extravagant in His devotion and tormented by her infidelities. These are all fundamentally important parts of the biblical portrait of God and quite irreconcilable with the view that He is emotionally inert.

Secondly, the idea that God is unaffected by occurrences outside Himself is inconsistent with the divine pity. Pity means by definition that one is stirred by the spectacle of human misery, temporal and spiritual. God cannot pity and yet remain unmoved. Indeed, for God to remain unmoved would raise serious questions as to His morality. The pain and grief which we feel when confronted with inhumanity, deprivation and squalor must have its counterpart (and indeed its source) in the God whose image we bear.

Thirdly, the idea that God is impassive and apathetic is inconsistent with the cross (which is the test of everything). We cannot say that Christ is our greatest word about God and yet say that we do not mean the crucified Christ. Nor can we say that the crucified *Christ* is the image of God and yet say that the *cross* is only a word about His human nature. It is precisely the crucified Christ who is the revelation; and what He reveals, in being crucified, is God.

Consequently, when the New Testament appeals to the moral force and constraint of Calvary, it is on the involvement of God the Father that it frequently focuses. The cross is the expression of *His* love and of *His* pity (John 3:16, Romans 8:32). *He* is the One whose conduct is the model of self-denial and cross-bearing. *He* is the One who bore the cost of redemption. Indeed, if He is so immobile and so passionless that Calvary cost Him nothing, all talk of Him must cease because our language about Him is meaningless. If Calvary was painless for Him, we are not made in His image and He does not love with our love. When Abraham offered Isaac, there was pain; when Jacob lost Joseph, there was pain; when David lost Absalom, there was pain. If things were different when God gave up His Son, then either He does not love His Son or His love is so radically different from ours as to be meaningless. We cling therefore to the belief that not only did God the Son suffer crucifixion but God the Father suffered the pain of delivering Him up. The Father was as really bereft as the Son was forsaken: and the Father suffered the loss of the Son as really as the Son suffered the loss of the Father. The Father did not suffer what the Son suffered (He was not crucified). But He suffered seeing the Son suffering and the even greater (and quite unfathomable) agony of being the One who had to bruise and forsake Him. He had to steel Himself not to respond to the terrible cry from the far country, 'My God, my God, why hast thou forsaken me?'

Yet Calvary was not an isolated moment of pain or pity in the experience of God. Its roots lay in the primeval and permanent concern of God for His creation. The cross does not inaugurate that concern. But it does show how deep and passionate it is, and how far God was prepared to go.

In the last analysis that concern is triune, shared equally by the Father, the Son and the Holy Spirit, as the history of the cross (involving the Father, the Son and the eternal Spirit) clearly testifies. The agony of each is different, yet equally real. And the resulting understanding of human grief is as much a reality for God the Father and God the Holy Spirit as it is for God the Son. The Trinity is touched with the feeling of our infirmities.

But even this cannot be the *last* word. The last word is the *risen* Christ, which means that for our doctrine of God the last word is not the *THEOLOGIA CRUCIS* but the *THEOLOGIA GLORIAE*. The God who is willing to go out to meet suffering is not willing to be defeated by it. It is His form (Philippians 2:6) to conquer it as surely as it is His form to take it. Indeed, it is only taken in order to its elimination. In the final outcome He is highly exalted and every knee bows (Philippians 2:9 f.). This means that the divine passion and the divine blessedness are not equal. They are asymmetrical, just as the suffering of the Christian and the glory of the Christian are asymmetrical (Romans 8:18). He is 'the blessed God' (1 Timothy 1:11) and He chooses to encounter suffering precisely to protect that blessedness (and, by implication, the blessedness of His creation). Probably, too, in a manner we can barely begin to perceive, He assimilates His *passion* into the very blessedness itself.

Classification

Several ways of classifying the attributes of God have won favour among theologians. Some have divided them into natural and moral; others into absolute and relative; others into original and derived; others into active and inactive; and yet others into communicable and incommunicable. None of these has much to commend it and certainly none is to be regarded as authoritative. Scripture nowhere attempts a classification; neither does such a representative statement as the Westminster Confession, which is content with an almost haphazard list of the perfections ascribed to God in the Bible (see Chapter II: I,II). All the suggested classifications are artificial and misleading, not least that which has been most favoured by Reformed theologians — the division into communicable and incommunicable attributes. The problem here is that the qualities we refer to as incommunicable adhere unalterably to those we refer to as communicable. For example, God is 'infinite, eternal and unchangeable' (*The Shorter Catechism*, Answer 4) and these are deemed to be incommunicable properties: and God is merciful, which is deemed to be a communicable property. But the mercy itself is 'infinite, eternal and unchangeable' and as such incommunicable. The same is true of all the other so-called communicable attributes such as the love, righteousness and faithfulness of God. On the other hand, to speak of omnipotence, omniscience and omnipresence as incommunicable is equally unsatisfactory. If we remove the prefix *omni* we are left simply with power, knowledge and presence, all of which have analogies in our own human existence.

As Karl Barth has pointed out (*Church Dogmatics*, Vol. II, Part I, p. 352), any exposition of the divine attributes 'has to come down in detail to a certain choice and grouping of concepts'. Whatever decision we make, our arrangement 'will not be able to appeal to any direct intimation of Holy Scripture nor to the voice of any sort of relative authority'. The only claim we make for the arrangement that follows is that it is convenient. *METHODUS EST ARBITRARIUS.*

CHAPTER ONE

IS THERE SUCH A THING AS AN ATHEIST?

Christian witness, whether lay or clerical, stands between the world and the Word. That means that to do it properly we have to understand both. We cannot evangelise unless we understand the Word: and we cannot evangelise unless we understand the world.

This second requirement is by no means as easy as it looks. The world, unlike the Word, is constantly changing, not least in the way it understands itself. Today, for example, we describe ourselves as a secular society. Our laws, our manners, our education and our culture are entirely divorced from religion. Our society is made up of atheists. At least, so everyone keeps telling us.

For the Christian communicator this creates enormous problems. How can we preach the gospel to atheists? Where can we find a point of contact with a man who believes nothing and to whom religious language and concepts make no sense (assuming there is such a man)? If he can make nothing of right and wrong, good and evil, what can talk of God, sin and salvation be but mumbo jumbo?

It is all very discouraging. But is it true? Is modern man an atheist? and are we to presuppose this in our evangelism?

Bible never proves the existence of God

When we turn to the Bible for answers to such questions we find, first of all, that it never, anywhere, tries to prove the existence of God. From Genesis to Revelation it simply assumes that God exists: and that men know that He exists.

We find, secondly, that when Paul preaches to the philosophers of Athens he takes it for granted that they believe in God. He certainly does not approach them as if they were atheists. Athens was not a secular city. On the contrary, it was only too religious, and Paul's approach is not to prove the existence of God but to proclaim the doctrine of creation, the equality of men, the certainty of judgment and the resurrection of Christ.

Thirdly, we find Paul in Romans 1: 18-32 telling us in so many words that God has revealed Himself to every human being: 'That which may be known of God is manifest in them;

for God has shown it to them'. Man, as Paul understands him, is surrounded with revelation because the visible world is by its very nature an unveiling of God: 'Since the creation, the invisible things of God are clearly seen, being understood through the things that are made, so that men are without excuse'.

This is a theme that goes back to the Old Testament, especially to Psalm 19: 'The heavens declare the glory of God and the skies proclaim the work of his hands'. In both Paul and the Psalmist stress is laid on the part played in this revelation by the static, external world. What we see speaks to us of God.

This has surely lost none of its force with the passing of the years. A generation which can peer into the structure of the atom and stand on the surface of the moon has more reason than even Paul to cry out, 'Oh! the depth of the wisdom and of the knowledge of God!'

But the revelation is not confined to man's static environment. It takes place, too, through the movements of history. This was particularly true of the history of Israel. Time and again God invaded the lives of His people and made Himself known. Experiences such as the Exodus lay at the very foundation of Israel's knowledge of God. But the Gentiles, too, experienced God's revelation through providence. Even when He allowed all the nations to walk in their own ways, 'He did not leave himself without witness: for he did good and gave you from heaven rains and fruitful seasons, satisfying your hearts with food and gladness' (Acts 14: 17). We have similar teaching from the lips of our Lord Himself in Matthew 5: 44 ff. God shows His love for His enemies by making His sun rise on the evil and on the good and sending rain on the just and on the unjust.

Even in Romans 1: 18-32 Paul is largely concerned with God's revelation through history rather than His revelation through creation. This is particularly true of the divine wrath, which is revealed not through the things that are made but in the life-style to which God has abandoned civilisation. The degeneracy, vice and idolatry which prevailed in the Roman empire were themselves demonstrations of the judicial alertness of God.

Nor is this revelation at all minimal. In fact it is remarkably full. From Romans 1: 18-32 alone we see that the things which are made proclaim the eternity, the power, the wrath, the judgment and the godhead of God. According to Acts 14: 17 and Matthew 5: 45ff., providence witnesses to God's love and goodness to all men, including His enemies. Such passages as Psalm 104: 24 and Proverbs 3:19 remind us of the disclosure of God's wisdom through creation.

Well-rounded impression of God

Obviously, then, men are not left with only a bare grasp of the existence of some kind of deity. As the Bible understands it what is given to all men is a well-rounded impression of God.

Two details in Paul's teaching in Romans One deserve special notice.

First, the phrase 'what may be known' of God. This strongly suggests that there is a range of truth which may *not* be known. God tells us only a little of what He knows about Himself. This is not because He wilfully withholds knowledge (as the Serpent suggests in Genesis 3:5) but because only a little is within man's grasp. This should cause no surprise. We have difficulty enough understanding the world itself and when we try to cram the findings of modern physics into our heads they burst (the debris falls out in apparently random masses of mathematics). The Creator Himself inevitably proves even more of a headache. Despite the eloquence of creation, the fulness of Scripture and the gains of two thousand years of theological reflection He remains a mystery. As Deuteronomy 29: 29 reminds us, there will always be 'secret things'. 'Man,' said Blaise Pascal, 'must not see nothing at all, nor must he see enough to think that he possesses God, but he must see enough to know that he has lost Him'.

The second interesting detail is the word *godhead* in the phrase 'his eternal power and godhead'. It occurs only here in the New Testament and its practical meaning is probably little different from *holiness*. When the creation points to the *godness* of God it is directing us to One mysterious, unmanageable and infinitely threatening, upon whom we are totally dependent and to whom we are unconditionally accountable. Sometimes this registers in our hearts as pure dread. We see this frequently, for example, in Wordsworth, a poet whose notion of God was far from Christian but who, nevertheless, had a profound sense of the Awesome. At one point in *The Prelude* he gives a memorable account of a childhood escapade in which, one dark night, he stole a boat and as he rowed 'into the silent lake' it seemed to him as if the huge peak which dominated the scene were striding after him.

But after I had seen
That spectacle, for many days, my brain
Worked with a dim and undetermined sense
Of unknown modes of being; o'er my thoughts
There hung a darkness, call it solitude
Or blank desertion.

But it is not always in feelings of dread and terror that the sense of the godness of God is reflected. Sometimes the emotion can be much more gentle, as in the almost too familiar words of Browning's *Bishop Blougram*:

Just when we're safest, there's a sunset-touch,
A fancy from a flower-bell, some one's death,
A chorus-ending from Euripides,
And that's enough for fifty hopes and fears
As old and new at once as nature's self.

The mood there is very different from the earlier quotation but the foundation is the same: in man there is an awareness of 'unknown modes of being' which can be stimulated into powerful action by a guilty conscience, a dark mountainscape or even by a flower-bell.

But isn't man blind?

But what is the use of such revelation if man cannot see? Isn't man blind? 'No!' says Paul, 'at this level man isn't blind at all.' Not only are the invisible perfections of God clearly revealed but they are clearly *seen.* They are *understood* by the things that are made (Romans 1.20). Man is so made that he cannot but infer from his environment the eternal power and godness of God. His mind (indeed, his whole psychology) is tuned in to the revelation which surrounds him. He is neither blind nor insensitive. The message actually gets through to him.

This is not to say, of course, that man makes proper use of this knowledge. On the contrary, he holds the truth in unrighteousness. Indeed, from mere observation of human life (and especially of man's religious practices) one could easily conclude that man knows little or nothing of the truth. If he does, why does he so often either not worship at all or worship completely worthless objects? Because, says Paul, he does not like to retain God in his knowledge (Romans 1: 28). Idolatrous man, falling down before birds and beasts and creeping things, is distorting the truth. Secular man, worshipping nothing (except himself) is suppressing the truth. It is quite wrong to ridicule general revelation on the ground of its being ineffectual. The gospel itself suffers the same fate, even when preached by an Isaiah or a Paul: 'Lord, who has believed our message?'

It is because he knows the truth that man's godlessness is inexcusable. Paul's argument is not that man's ignorance is inexcusable because revelation is so clear, but that man's religious behaviour (or lack of it) is inexcusable because he is *not ignorant.* In refusing to bow the knee to God he is keeping the lid on truth which wells up, demanding a response, within himself. In the words of Calvin, 'Men court darkness ... stifle the light of nature and intentionally stupify themselves' (*Institutes,* Bk. I, Ch. IV. 1,2.)

A sense of deity on every heart

If our understanding of Paul is correct, there is no such thing as an atheist. This has certainly been the traditional view of Reformed theology. To quote Calvin, 'God has endued all men with some sense of His godhead', with the result that 'a sense of deity is inscribed on every heart'. (*Ibid,* Bk. I, Ch III. 1) Moreover, this knowledge is indelible. Man never loses it: 'Although men struggle with their own convictions and would fain not only banish God from their minds but from heaven also, their stupefaction is never so complete as to prevent them from being dragged occasionally before the divine tribunal' (Ibid. Bk. I, Ch. IV. 2). This agrees with what Paul says at the close of Romans One: even when men sink to the very bottom of the moral abyss, not only engaging in perverted practices themselves but hero-worshipping those who excel in them, they carry with them a sense of the judgment of God (Romans 1:32). 'Still,' wrote Calvin, 'the conviction that there is some deity continues to exist, like a plant which can never be completely eradicated, though so corrupt that it is only capable of producing the worst of fruit' (*Ibid,* Bk I, Ch. IV. 4).

Practical implications

All this has three obvious practical implications.

First, we can never accept men's claim that they are atheists or agnostics. Such a claim contradicts what the Bible tells us about human nature. Wherever we go we have to assume that there is a divinely implanted awareness of God in every human soul.

Secondly, we can take it for granted that basic religious concepts such as God, eternity, holiness, sin and judgment are meaningful to all men and women. To begin our evangelism by trying to get behind this framework (by setting out to prove, for example, that God exists) is to walk into a philosophical maze. We must not confuse knowledge of God (religion) with knowledge of how we know Him (epistemology).

Finally, all Christian witness must start from the assumption that 'the seed of religion' exists in every human heart. This was certainly where Paul began with the Athenians. He did not try to make them religious. The evidence that they were already religious was all around him in the temples and altars and other priestly paraphernalia of the city. All men have a sense of the holy. All men have a feeling of dependence. All have God's law within their hearts. All know that they are answerable to God. It is not our calling to instil these instincts in men. Our responsibility is to build on the foundation which God has already laid.

CHAPTER TWO

WHAT IS GOD?

The question, What is God? is ambiguous. It may mean, What is He *essentially (quid)*? Or it may mean, What is He like (*qualis*)? The closest Scripture comes to answering the question in its first form is in the statement, 'God is a spirit', (John 4:24). It is important to note the limitation of this assertion, however. God is unique. He is *sui generis*. There is only one God and He may not be categorised. He is not one of a class. There is no other form of being with which the being of God is continuous or in terms of which His nature can be understood. The only adequate answer to the question, 'What is God essentially?' is the tautology, God is godhead. The essence of God is deity.

Yet God chooses to describe Himself as spirit and the immediate effect of this is to categorise Him, because He is not the only spirit. Men are spirits and angels are spirits. This is therefore only a partial and very inadequate description of the nature of God. Why, then, is it used? Basically because our thinking about God must be analogical. We can only conceive of Him and describe Him in terms of concepts and categories familiar from our own experience. *Spirit* is the highest category known to man. It does not describe God exhaustively or even adequately. But we have no higher analogy and it does render the very important service of reminding us that we are not to conceive of the Creator in terms inferior to those we apply to ourselves.

The spirituality of God means, first of all, that He is immaterial and incorporeal. Jehovah, unlike the gods of the nations, did not have a form or similitude. He was not flesh, but spirit. He was invisible and intangible, immeasurable and uncontainable. He had no bodily parts or passions. He had no physical needs or dependence and consequently, no frailty. He fainted not, neither became weary. The stern, uncompromising prohibition of the making or worshipping of images or even using them as aids in devotion reflects the divine jealousy on this point. Here, too, we have the most obvious distinction between man as spirit and God as spirit. Man is corporeal spirit (although he can exist incorporeally). God is pure spirit.

The spirituality of God means, secondly, that He is to be conceived of in terms of personality. He is an individual distinct from His creation, free, intelligent, self-conscious and affectionate. This may seem very elementary, but in actual fact such a conception of God has seldom, if ever, been attained except by those religions which are rooted in the Old Testament revelation — Judaism, Christianity and Islam. It is distinctive of biblical religion and indeed constitutes a frontal challenge both to the pagan theology of the ancient East and the philosophical theology of our own day. God is not to be identified with any physical object. He is not a tree-god, or a mountain-god. He is not the sun or the moon or any of the heavenly bodies. Nor is He to be identified with any of the forces of nature. He is not a storm-god or a thunder-god or, like Baal and Asherah, a fertility-god. Nor is He to be conceived of in purely intellectualist, abstract terms. He is not the First Cause or the Prime Mover or the Absolute — terms hopelessly inadequate to describe One who knows, who is jealous, who loves and who is provoked.

This abstractionism was given a new lease of life in the theology of Tillich, Bultmann and Robinson (who unfairly attributed it to Bonhoeffer as well). Negatively, those scholars were concerned to dissociate themselves from the theistic concept of God as at once personal and transcendent. 'We are reaching the point,' wrote Robinson, 'at which the whole conception of a God 'out there' is itself becoming more of a hindrance than a help' (*Honest to God*, SCM Press Ltd., London, 1966, p. 15). More broadly, the plea represented just one note among many in Bultmann's strident call for demythologisation: the whole conception of the world which is presupposed in the preaching of Jesus and in the New Testament generally must be abandoned because 'modern science does not believe that the course of nature can be interrupted or, so to speak, perforated, by supernatural powers' (*Jesus Christ and Mythology*, SCM Press, London, 1964, p.15). We were urged to abandon orthodoxy for the view that God was not *a* being or *another* being, but was *being itself*. There were many variations on the theme, none of them much more illuminating. God was the ground of being. He was the depth at the centre of life. He was our ultimate concern. He was what we take seriously without reservation. At the same time there was a unanimous concern to retain the Christian emphasis that God is love. Henceforth, however, 'God is love' means, 'Being itself is love'; or, conversely, 'love is the ground of our being'; or, again, it means that in love one comes in touch with the fundamental reality in the universe.

It is difficult to see how this concept of deity can be assimilated into Christianity. It is rooted in rejection of the Christian rule of faith and represents, in its development, a deliberate repudiation of the most fundamental and most distinctive elements of the biblical tradition. Morever, it is inconsistent, even in its own *prima facie* radicalism. By what criteria do we decide to salvage from the wreck of revelation the concept, 'God is love' and at the same time abandon all else? The authority for the fact of such love is precisely the same as for the concept of 'God out there,' namely, 'Thus saith the Lord.'

It is wholly remarkable, given the phenomena - given the facts of sin and suffering - that the one notion retained from Scripture as being in some way self-evident, is that God is love. In fact, the retention of this emphasis on the divine love renders this whole new approach absurd and self-contradictory. 'What does it mean,' asks Lesslie Newbigin, 'to say that love is the ground of our being, to which we ultimately come home, if we have first denied the existence of the Lover? What is love when there is no Lover?' (*Honest Religion for Secular Man*, S.C.M. Press, London, 1969, p.88). We cannot reject the notion of God as transcendent-personal and yet hope to retain the idea that love is His very heart. Such a concept can only survive in the soil in which it germinated — in the Hebrew-Christian tradition, committed beyond recall to the doctrine that God is a being distinct from the universe, knowing it, loving it and provoked by it. Such a God may be infinitely more than what we mean by personal. He is certainly not less.

The question of what is meant by personality is not, as such, faced in Scripture. In its application to God, however, it must include at least the following elements.

First, God relates to us as one human being relates to another. To use Martin Buber's terminology, our relationship with Him is not one of *I — It* but one of *I — Thou*. (*I and Thou*, T. & T. Clark, Edinburgh, 2nd edition, 1959). He is not a thing to us, nor we to Him. He is One who comes to meet us, approaching us and saying, 'My name is...' He speaks and He listens. He commits Himself to us and gets involved with us. He shares. He knows. He commands. He loves. He is provoked, grieved and propitiated. He rejoices.

Secondly, God is self-determining. He formulates plans. He makes decisions. He initiates action and carries it through. He is not a helpless component in a relentless causal nexus but an independent agent, immanent in the sequence of events and always involved in it: but never imprisoned by it. Men and angels exercise a similar voluntary agency. But theirs is analogical, derived from God, dependent upon Him and accountable to Him. His agency is primary and archetypal, expressing itself in the inimitable acts of creation, providence and redemption. In an utterly unconditional sense, He does according to His will (Daniel 4:35).

Thirdly, God possesses self-consciousness. Like man, He can look at Himself, evaluatively and reflectively. Indeed, this is the presupposition of all divine reflection. Revelation is God talking about God (letting us know a little of what He knows about Himself). But it is possible only because, first of all, God reflects upon Himself and so knows Himself that to Himself there is in His nature no hidden depth of incomprehensibility or ambiguity.

The personalness of God is closely linked in Christian theology with the doctrine of the trinity, although, again, Scripture does not reflect on the connection between them. So far as we can see in our present state of knowledge, self-consciousness can only exist where there is *another* of whom one is aware as distinct from oneself. Similarly, love presupposes *another* to love. This otherness is provided in the revelation of God as triune. God is one. But He is not solitary, because the Son is always with the Father and the Father and the Son are always with the Holy Spirit. Each is conscious of Himself as *I* in the fellowship of the other. Each says *Thou* to the other.

This element in God's revelation of Himself is in the highest degree helpful and illuminating. But the way the doctrine is verbalised in Christian orthodoxy leaves us with the problem that the word *person* bears two different senses. God is a person: and each member of the trinity is a person. God is personal: and each member of the trinity is personal. This means, to quote W.G.T. Shedd (*Dogmatic Theology*, Vol. I, p.193) that 'the personality of the Essence or Godhead must be distinguished from that of a Person in the Essence or Godhead.' The one God, Jehovah, has self-consciousness. He is an I. He knows. He wills. He loves. He is conscious of Himself as one agent and as one God. To quote Shedd again: 'The three hypostatical consciousnesses make one self-consciousness'. God is conscious of Himself as triune. His self-consciousness is trinal.

Yet there is also a particular individual consciousness and self-consciousness of each person of the eternal trinity. The

Father is conscious of Himself as the Father, who begets. The Son is conscious of Himself as the Son, who is begotten. And the Spirit is conscious of Himself as the Spirit, who proceeds.

Prima facie, then, we can speak of God as simultaneously one person and three persons. But this is both confusing and misleading. *Person* does not mean the same when applied to the one God as it does when applied to each member of the trinity separately. The one, triune God is a numerically distinct individual being. A person *in* the trinity is not. If the Father, the Son and the Spirit were numerically distinct we should have three gods, and thus violate the most fundamental doctrine of Jehovahism: 'Jehovah our God is one Jehovah' (Deuteronomy 6:4).

Granted the limits of our terminology — that we speak only in order not to be silent — there appears to be no way that this confusion can be wholly avoided. All we can do is ensure that the necessary distinctions are clear in our own minds. The one, living God is a person. The divine essence or nature is personal. The Father is a person, the Son is a person and the Spirit is a person.

CHAPTER THREE

HIS GREAT NAME

Further light is cast on the question of the nature of God by the names applied to Him in Scripture. The primary name is *El*, with its derivatives *Eloah* and *Elohim* and the compound forms *El Shaddai* and *El Elyon*.

The etymology of the word *El* is obscure, but the most widely accepted suggestion is that it is derived from a root meaning 'to be strong or powerful', and thus portrays God as *the mighty one*, and, by implication, as *the leader*. He is a being of infinite, overwhelming power, before whom the proper emotions are fear and dread. In keeping with this, when Christ comes as the incarnate revelation of God, His life is distinguished by a great series of mighty acts destructive of the works of the devil. Similarly, when Paul describes the content of the revelation of God given through the things that are made he does so in terms of 'eternal power and godhead' (Romans 1: 20). That is the primary impression made by the presence of God on the consciousness of man.

The actual usage of the name *El* is even more instructive. It occurs frequently as a component of proper names, both of places and people. As examples of the former we may instance *Bethel* and *Penuel*. There are innumerable examples of the latter — *Ishmael, Elijah, Elisha, Shelumiel, Nethanel, Eliah, Elishama, Gamaliel* and *Pagiel*. This fact serves as a counterpoise to the emphasis on the power, majesty and threateningness of God. It associates Him with people and places and thus portrays Him as an involved God. He is not only transcendent, but immanent. He is not to be conceived of deistically as a God afar off, but as One moving — and moving helpfully — in the sphere of man's social and moral needs. He sees. He hears. He speaks. He delivers. He leads. He destroys. He heals. He is present within space-time history in a whole series of observable acts — not only quietly working all things according to the counsel of His will, but on occasion causing His power to erupt into the world of phenomena, sometimes in compassion and sometimes in judgment.

Yet another dimension is added by the practice of naming *El* after the patriarchs in such phrases as the God of Abraham, the God of your fathers, and the God of Isaac and of Jacob. This carries us beyond the idea of mere involvement to the more radical and startling idea of commitment: 'I shall be God to thee and to thy seed after thee' (Genesis 17:7). It is in this commitment of God to a people that the Exodus, the supreme Old Testament example of the beneficent exercise of power, is rooted: 'God heard their groaning, and God remembered his covenant with Abraham, with Isaac and with Jacob' (Exodus 2:24). This means that although the idea of power is primary yet that power is not going to operate arbitrarily. It is bounded by a whole series of covenants (*berithim*) which assure men of a certain stability and predictability in the workings of divine providence. The most basic of these was the covenant with Noah (Genesis 9: 8-17). This constituted a commitment on God's part not only to a chosen race, but to the whole of mankind and indeed to 'every living creature that is with you, the fowl, the cattle and every beast of the earth'. It promised a framework of general stability within which man should confidently set about replenishing the earth. The importance of this cannot be overestimated, especially in an age when ecological fears tempt men to abdicate from the responsibilities involved in the creation-mandates.

In the covenant with Abraham the idea of commitment is carried even further. God pledges Himself in the fulness of affection, power and prerogative to a particular people. He will *be* for them. In the great phrase of Jeremiah, He becomes the *portion* of Jacob (Jeremiah 10: 16). The full implications of this appear only in the New Testament, where we see that God's commitment means, at last, 'He loved me and gave himself for me' (Galatians 2: 20). It is scarcely possible to rise higher, even in conception, than this — unless, perhaps, in the immeasurable grace of the words of God incarnate: 'And the glory which thou gavest me I have given them' (John 17: 22). Here the idea of commitment passes over into the idea of communion, in which the church, as a joint heir with Christ, shares His status and His privileges.

One further peculiarity relating to the name *Elohim* may be noted. This is by far the most common designation of God in the Old Testament, occurring some 2,300 times. The interesting thing is that it is a plural form habitually used with verbs or adjectives in the singular. This phenomenon — a plural form for a single deity — is not altogether unique to Israel, but it is highly significant nevertheless. It is a plural of majesty (or, perhaps more accurately, of intensity) the effect of which is to expand and reinforce the original concept. In this case it emphasises that Israel's God is *El* in a pre-eminent sense. He is the might *par excellence*, possessed of an absolute plenitude of power and energy. He is the perfect representative of godhead. He is not just an individual *el*, but the sum of all the gods, the One whose existence rules out that of all other deities. This peculiar form is thus an expression of Israel's monotheism, as appears from Psalm 100:3. 'Jehovah, He is Elohim'. He is the epitome of all creative power and might, possessing, in New Testament phraseology, all the fulness (*pleroma*) of godhead.

Jehovah

Alongside the generally Semitic word *El* and its derivatives must be set the distinctively Israelitish designation, *Jehovah*.

Its meaning has been fixed for Christian theology by the revelation given in Exodus 3: 14. 'And God said unto Moses, *I AM THAT I AM*: and he said, Thus shalt thou say unto the children of Israel. I AM hath sent me unto you.' This revelation has not satisfied the curiosity or controlled the researches of those who do not share the historic Christian attitude to the Old Testament, and the quest for an allegedly more satisfactory etymology continues. No convincing alternative has been proposed, however, and the consensus of academic opinion is fairly expressed by Eichrodt, who writes, 'The most natural interpretation remains that which equates the Tetragrammaton with 'He is', 'He exists', 'He is present' (*Theology of the Old Testament*, S.C.M. Press, London, 1969, Volume One, p.189). *EHYEH*, translated 'I am' by the Authorised Version, is an archaic form of the imperfect tense of the verb *to be* and, in accordance with the nature of the imperfect tense in Hebrew, should be translated as a future. Consequently, the primary meaning of *EHYEH* is, 'I shall be', and the primary meaning of *JHVH* is, 'He will be'. One further interesting fact should be noted. Exodus 3:14 is translated by the Septuagint, 'I am *ho on*', literally, 'I am the being one'. Whatever the merits of this as a translation it demands the attention of Christian theology because it is taken over by the book of Revelation as one of the great designations of God (see Revelation 1: 4, 1:8).

The connection between the divine name Jehovah and the idea of being is, therefore, clearly established. But what are the distinctive emphases?

The first point, surely, is that, as distinct from every other pretended deity, Jehovah *is*. He has being. He is there. No truth is more important than this. The idols are nothing. They are vanities. But Jehovah is a true and living God.

Secondly, He is the *being* one, as distinct from the *becoming* one. To say that the idea of self-existence is already present in Exodus 3:14 may be an over-statement. But as the cumulative movement of revelation pours more and more content into the name this concept is frequently brought into prominence. The title *the being one*, upon which the later revelation places its imprimatur, surely implies this. With particular reference to God the Son, this truth is brought out with great force and beauty in the prologue to John's Gospel: 'In the beginning *was* the Word and the Word *was* with God and the Word *was* God'. In each instance of the reiterated verb the tense used is the imperfect, indicative of on-going being: 'In the beginning, the Word was already in being'. The effect is heightened by a deliberate two-fold contrast. The being of the Word is contrasted, first of all, with the *creation* of all other being: 'All things were made by Him'. The verb used here, *egeneto*, indicates *becoming* as distinct from *being*. And the tense is not the imperfect, but the aorist, pointing here to a definite event. In the beginning God the Word was already in being. But in that same beginning all other things came into being. And they came into being through Him. He is the unoriginated Author of all being, the unmade Maker of all made things. But the being of the Word is also contrasted with the event of the incarnation: 'The Word was made flesh'. Here again we have *becoming* as distinct from *being*: and here also we have an aorist as distinct from an imperfect tense. In the beginning, the Word was already in being. But, at a particular moment (when the fulness of the times was come) He became or was made flesh and pitched His tabernacle (temporarily) among us.

Thirdly, the name Jehovah highlights the on-going inexhaustibleness of the divine being. He will be. He will be the being one. These are, indeed, the primary ideas. But they again, are deliberately heightened by the context in which the name is revealed. For example, the name is surely closely related to the vision of the burning bush described in Exodus 3: 1-6. Moses himself draws our attention to the significance of this theophany when he says, 'I will now turn aside and see this great sight, *why the bush is not burnt*' (Exodus 3: 3). The bush is not burnt. That is the primary thing. Doubtless there are other nuances. Fire is frequently a symbol of divine holiness, purity and awesomeness, and such an inexplicable conflagration in the heart of the desert was, as Moses expressly says, 'a great sight'.

But the kernel of the revelation is not so much that God burns awesomely or threateningly or gloriously as that He burns unconsumed. He is. He was. He will be the being One, inexhaustibly. As *El* He is power or energy, august yet benign. As Jehovah, that energy burns unconsumedly. The same idea occurs in one of Isaiah's great perorations: 'Hast thou not known? hast thou not heard? the everlasting God, Jehovah, the creator of the ends of the earth, fainteth not, neither is weary' (Isaiah 40: 28).

At the same time the disclosure of the name Jehovah is deliberately related to what God has shown Himself to be in the past. The God of the burning bush is specifically identified as 'the God of thy fathers, the God of Abraham, the God of Isaac and the God of Jacob' (Exodus 3: 6). Again in Exodus 3: 14-15 the two kinds of designation are brought together: 'Thus shalt thou say unto the children of Israel, I AM hath sent me unto you' (verse 14), followed in verse 15 by, 'Thus shalt thou say unto the children of Israel, Jehovah, God of your fathers, the God of Abraham, the God of Isaac and the God of Jacob has sent me unto you'. The new name does not mean a break with the revelation of the past. On the contrary, it is precisely the glory of the God of their fathers which is brought out in the designation Jehovah. The past is the basis of the reassurance implicit in the new name. Jehovah means, 'He will be'. But what will He be? He will be as He was to their fathers. That is the core of His immutability. It is not a metaphysical, abstract immutability but an irrevocable commitment to His people. He has been the God of their fathers. He will be the God of their seed. Commitment is His very heart, what He has been and what He will be. The bush not only burns inexhaustibly. It burns for Israel. 'I will be God for thee', was the very kernel of the promise. His resources, His energy, His prerogatives and all the workings of His providence are for His people. He rides upon the heavens precisely 'in thy help', (Deuteronomy 33: 26).

New depths of meaning

While it is true, however, that the name Jehovah attracts to itself at once all the glory of the previous revelation it is no less true that the full content of its meaning remains to be supplied by the on-going process of redemption. The conquest of the land, the experiences of David, the acts of Elijah and Elisha and the messages of the great prophets all add new depths of meaning to the Name. The process culminates in Christ. The most basic of all Christian confessions is, 'Jesus is Jehovah'. This means that all the glory and honour accruing to the name Jehovah through the previous centuries of revelation are immediately declared to be appropriate to Jesus. The name, attributes, prerogatives and functions of Jehovah are His. But it also means that Jehovah cannot be fully or properly understood apart from Jesus. He is Jehovah. He is the mirror of deity, the image of God, the form of God and the glory of God.

What is especially significant is the obvious determination of the New Testament to focus attention on condescending, redemptive grace at those very moments when it points out most clearly that Jesus is the pre-eminent revelation of Jehovah. One of the clearest instances of this is John 1: 14, 'We beheld his glory, glory as of the only-begotten of the Father, full of grace and truth'. Jesus is the glory of the Father. But the glory of Jesus is the glory of grace and truth. Consequently, the glory of the Father is the glory of grace and truth. We find the same idea in Philippians 2: 6, which represents Jesus as pre-existing 'in the form of God'. In classical usage the word *form* (morphe) indicates the essential nature of a thing. In the Septuagint it is used virtually interchangeably with *image* and *glory* . Either way, Paul's statement in Philippians 2: 6 indicates the possession by the pre-incarnate Son of all that constitutes deity. But there follows the astounding statement that He made Himself of no reputation (literally, He emptied Himself), taking the form of a servant, the appearance of a man and, at last, the accursed death of the cross.

This means at once that self-emptying, humiliation, incarnation, obedience and even crucifixion cannot be inconsistent with the form of God. They will seem to be and be deemed to be, much as Peter said to the Lord, 'Thou shalt never wash my feet', assuming that the form of God cannot co-exist with the form of a servant. But the fact of the incarnation shows very clearly that what God is is not contradicted by humiliation, suffering and obedience.

Surely, however, we may go even further. This humiliation must have its basis in the very being of God. It is rooted in what He is and expresses what He is. Indeed, it expresses His very heart. Reverting to John 1: 14, we may say that grace (loving-kindness) is His glory. It is His essential nature. The form of God, as seen in Philippians 2: 5-11, does not consist in self-assertion, but in self-renunciation. Doubtless, this whole complex of ideas must be handled with great care. We must not obscure the voluntariness of the humiliation. It did not flow from His essence in the sense of being inevitable. Moreover, the incarnate Jesus does not present us with an unqualified picture of weakness and meekness. There are moments of awesome might, moments of unveiled numinousness and moments when it is very plain that He is of purer eye than to condone iniquity. But His very presence in human form and in the stream of human experience is redolent of condescension. And when His glory is later recalled it is precisely here that it is seen to have been concentrated. It was the glory of grace. His grandeur was that, although rich, for our sake He became poor. The point is not that He is gracious. It is that this is His glory. The love which prompted to humiliation is His very heart. Here we may agree with Karl Barth: 'We cannot refuse to accept the humiliation and lowliness and supremely the obedience of Christ as the dominating moment in our conception of God' (*Church Dogmatics*, Vol. IV, Part I p. 199).

One other fact connected with the revelation of Exodus 3: 1-18 ought not to be ignored. Moses' immediate reaction when he sees the burning bush is to say, 'I will now turn aside and see this great sight.' This resolution is deliberately opposed by God: 'Draw not nigh hither: put off thy shoes from off thy feet, for the place whereon thou standest is holy ground.' God is not simply a great sight, the object of speculative curiosity. The revelation of His glory and the whole theological process which legitimately follows from it is holy ground. We cannot stand as superiors over God or His Word. We may not coldly and detachedly analyse and collate the great self-revealing deeds and utterances of Jehovah. We may not theologise without emotion and commitment. The doctrine must thrill and exhilarate. It must humble and cast down. Our researches must be punctuated with frequent cries of, 'Oh! the depth!' and even periodically abandoned so that the pent-up emotions of our hearts may find relief in expressions of wonder, love and praise. Theology has lost its way, and, indeed its very soul, if it cannot say with John, 'I fell at his feet as dead' (Rev. 1: 17).

CHAPTER FOUR

THE POWER OF GOD

The fact of divine omnipotence is already underlined in the biblical designations of God. As we have seen, the most basic of these, *EL*, is derived from a root meaning *strength*. This concept is intensified in such names as *El GIBBOR* (the mighty God, Isaiah 9:6) and *EL SHADDAI* (God almighty, Genesis 17:1). The latter name appears in the New Testament in the form *PANTOKRATOR* (literally 'the all-holding one'). These are not distinctively Hebrew or biblical names. They were in general use among the Semitic peoples and this underlines the fact that the divine attribute of power is one of those perfections which is disclosed in general revelation. His eternal power is clearly seen even by the pagan, being understood from the things that are made (Romans 1:20). We should also note that the word *power* (*DUNAMIS*) by itself is used as a designation of God in Mark 14:62, 'You will see the Son of man seated at the right hand of (the) power, and coming with the clouds of heaven'. This is a reminder of the very close identification of the idea of power with the concept of God in the minds of the biblical writers. This is equally true, of course, in the case of holiness (Isaiah 6:3) and love (1 John 4:8).

God is almighty. His power extends over the whole universe, which is so entirely at His disposal that He can do within it whatever He wills; and as the Creator of all other powers He stands over them and holds them in His hand. They are wholly dependent on Him. They constitute no threat to Him. Nor do they impose limitations. God can do whatever He wills, so that He Himself is the measure of all possibilities. He is not limited by any extraneous, independent or competing force or by the data or structures of any situation.

Qualifications

The assertion of absolute divine power must, however, be qualified in at least three directions.

First of all, the power of God operates under the control of the divine character. God, to use the terminology of John MacQuarrie, is not limited by the 'factical' situation confronting Him. 'God's omnipotence means that He Himself, not any factical situation, is the source and also the horizon of all possibilities' (*Principles of Christian Theology,* S.C.M. Press,

London, 1971, p. 189). But from the list of possibilities open to Him we must exclude everything which is 'inconsistent with the structures and dynamics of God Himself'. God is love, God is holiness, God is righteousness, and He never asserts or exercises His power in a manner inconsistent with these. The power is always *His*, rooted in His wisdom, righteousness and grace.

Secondly, the operation of God's power is modified by the covenant. The gods of the nations were capricious and unpredictable and their devotees lived in constant dread of their malevolent and irrational intrusion into their daily lives. But this was not true of Israel's God. He was reliable and predictable and stood in a stable relationship both with the world and with His people. As a subjective fact of the Hebrew consciousness, this was not due exclusively to their clearer apprehension of the divine character. It was very largely the result of their awareness that all God's dealings with men occurred within the framework of a covenant. This was true even of His primeval relationship with man. God had made a promise to Adam, perfectly clear as to its conditions, and His power would never be put forth in contradiction of it. Similarly, after the Flood, God's relationship with the whole human race is placed on an explicit covenant-footing (Genesis 9: 8ff). His power will never again (until the end) erupt in universal judgment. He will never again curse the ground for man's sake. Nor will He ever again destroy every living thing. Instead, God promises that, in general, man will enjoy the benefits of a stable, predictable and productive environment: 'Seedtime and harvest, and cold and heat, and summer and winter and day and night will not cease' (Genesis 8: 22).

This predictability of the divine power, operating within the stable framework of a promise, culminates in God's covenant with Abraham, modified, but not abrogated, by the Sinaitic covenant and re-affirmed in the new covenant ratified by the blood of Christ. God becomes His people's God: bound to them and committed to effecting their redemption. Consequently, His power will never turn on them destructively. It is *for* them, constantly operating in their interest. Christ is the last word in this connection. He is given as a covenant to the people (Isaiah 42: 6), so that all the promises of God are yea and amen in Him (2 Corinthians 1:20). God's power will never operate in a way that contradicts the pledge as to the divine nature and intention given in Christ.

Thirdly, the absoluteness of the divine power is qualified by the fact that God is not the only power. As Creator, He is the source of all power. But other powers and agents exist which, although not independent, are yet distinct. To deny this is to land ourselves in the kind of pantheism typical of Islam, according to which God is the author equally of both good and evil, and even the illusion of choice present to the human mind is His creation. This attitude is reproduced to an intriguing extent in the determinism characteristic of the behavioural sciences, which too often portray man as the plaything of circumstances and the prisoner of heredity and environment. Over against this, Reformed theology asserts the status of men as distinct agents, possessing by divine gift their own free and effective creativity. God has foreordained whatever comes to pass, but that does not take away 'the liberty or contingency of second causes'. In fact it establishes them (*Westminster Confession*, III.I). God has foreordained freedom.

The Demonstration of Power

The primary demonstration of divine power is the work of creation. Time and again the writers of Scripture appeal to this as the measure of God's energy and competence. 'Lift up your eyes on high!' cries Isaiah, 'and behold who hath created these things, that bringeth out their host by number: he calleth them all by names by the greatness of his might, because he is strong in power' (Isaiah 40:26). This again is why it is so absurd to think of God as spent or exhausted: 'The Creator of the ends of the earth fainteth not, neither is weary' (Isaiah 40: 28). According to Psalm 100: 3, this is the very meaning of godhead: 'Know that Jehovah is God: it is he that made us and not we ourselves'. Similarly in Psalm 121:2 this is the basis of our confidence in God's power to keep us: 'My help comes from Jehovah, who made heaven and earth'. The same attitude is reflected in Romans 8:39, 'I am persuaded that no creature (nothing created) is able to separate us from the love of God in Christ Jesus'.

The basic biblical idea of creation is expressed in the Hebrew word *BARA*. This word does not in and of itself carry the meaning 'to create out of nothing'. But it is very significant that it is never used in Scripture except to describe a divine activity. It is something man cannot emulate and in which he cannot share. Furthermore it always refers to the production of something which is new, either in matter or in form. Again, it is never followed by an accusative of the materials used: a fact which emphasises that in this creative activity God operated with absolute freedom, unhindered by any recalcitrance on the part of the elements He was manipulating. Nothing external to Himself inhibited the operation. We should also note that even in the first chapter of Genesis the word *BARA* is used sparingly. It is used of the primary act of creation out of nothing (Genesis 1:1), of the creation of conscious life (Genesis 1:21) and of the creation of man (Genesis 1:27). This strongly underlines the pre-eminent dignity of the divine creativity. It is not something in which God is constantly or habitually engaged. Only certain of His acts are to be placed in this category. There is a point at which God rests from His creative activity and pronounces the result 'very good' (Genesis 1:31). Certainly the Father still works (John 5:17). But these are works of providence concerned not with the origination of something new but with the preservation and government of that which already exists.

The work of creation is effected by the word of divine power. This is clearly indicated in the Genesis narrative with its insistence on 'God said!' as the primary instrumentality. It is underlined in later biblical references to creation. The Writer to the Hebrews declares, for example, that 'the worlds were framed by the word of God' (Hebrews 11: 3). Peter writes to the same effect: 'By the word of God the heavens were of old, and the earth standing out of the water and in the water' (2 Peter 3: 5). The universe was conceived in the mind of God. There the idea was born. To that extent God's creativity is analogous to man's. But the manner in which the idea is translated into reality is utterly different. God did not manipulate or manufacture. He spoke the universe into being, so that 'by the word of Jehovah were the heavens made, and all the host of them by the breath of his mouth' (Psalm 33: 6).

The matter is slightly complicated, however, by the fact that Genesis clearly indicates two levels of divine creativity.

First, there is *immediate* creation, creation out of nothing in the strict sense, using no pre-existing materials. By this, God spoke the elements and primary particles of mass and energy into being. In the same way, probably, God created light. In the same way, too, He created the human soul.

But the word *BARA* is also used to describe acts of *mediate* creation, where God originates new modes of being by organising and imparting form to pre-existent materials. In mediate creation God operates through second causes, as appears in such statements as, 'Let the earth bring forth!' or, 'Let the waters bring forth!' (Genesis 1: 24, 20). We find the same mediateness in the creation of man: 'And Jehovah God formed man of the dust of the ground' (Genesis 2: 7). It appears, again, in the creation of woman: 'And the rib which Jehovah God had taken from man, made (builded) he a woman, and brought her to the man' (Genesis 2: 22).

Both these modes of activity — mediate and immediate — are equally *creation*. The life-forms described in Genesis 1: 21 are brought forth by the waters and yet they were specifically said to have been created. Similarly, man was formed of the dust of the ground and yet he too is specifically said to have been created (Genesis 2: 7).

We should also bear in mind that mediate creation may have involved very long processes; that certain records of the course of events involved in these processes may be accessible to us today; and that these records may be researched by specialists in the various scientific disciplines. There is indisputably both a theological and a palaeontological record of the sequence of creation events and each is a legitimate subject of human research. The theologian especially must bear in mind that the existence of the stratigraphical and fossil record gives the scientist the right to pronounce from his own point of view on the early development of life. Both theologian and scientist, however, must be careful to avoid the fallacy of what Professor Donald Mackay called 'nothing-buttery' (*The Clockwork Image*, Inter-Varsity Press, London, 1976, p. 40ff). It is true that fish and insects and reptiles are such as they are described by the fossil record. But it is not true that they are 'nothing but' that. Neither the Genesis record nor the fossil-record, nor indeed both of them together, is a complete description. Each must be supplemented by the other and by the insights of many other disciplines. Indeed, only to the mind of God is there present an exhaustive knowledge of molluscs and vertebrates, of quadrupeds and men.

Within the creation-process as described in Genesis there is a clear progression. The features of the chaos described in Genesis 1: 2 are successively eliminated. The darkness is dispelled by the creation of light, the presupposition of order and life. The formlessness is eliminated by the creation of the firmament and the separation of land and sea. The emptiness is overcome by the creation of life. But as the sequence moves from light to order to life, so it moves from the creation of the more elementary life-forms to the more complex. Vegetable life appears (verse 11) before animal life (verse 20). The first animals to be created are those of the sea followed by birds or insects and then by the reptiles and the beasts of the earth (verses 24, 25). Finally, God creates man (verse 27).

The general fact of progression is confirmed by the palaeontological record. The oldest strata contain fossils of the most primitive life-forms, while the more recent contain the remains of the most sophisticated. Both scientist and theologian agree that the progression culminates in man; and both also agree that he has appeared only very recently. He is of yesterday.

Yet we must not be blind to the fact that there are wide divergences between the teaching of Scripture (as the Christian feels bound to interpret it in his present state of knowledge) and the views of the vast majority of contemporary scientists. Today's consensus geology and biology give a virtually unthinking allegiance to the idea of a purely naturalistic development according to which the various forms of existence emerged successively out of potentialities latent in the universe itself. They also hold that the biological progression is determined simply by the principle of natural selection, constraining the myriads of life-forms to effect mutations in themselves (either so that they became better fitted to survive or even so that they became transformed into completely new species).

While the Christian is committed to the doctrine of mediate and progressive creation he is bound to take a radically different view of the energy which sustains it and the principle which guides it. God is at every point the Creator. There is no process, no progress and no development apart from Him. Every new thing, every modification and every advance occurs only by His *express will* and is effected directly by His power. New forms of existence do not emerge autonomously and spontaneously out of the inherent potentialities of those already in being. God speaks the new into existence. Moreover, in the Christian view, the rate of *progression is not uniform* nor are the mutations involved in the emergence of new life-forms imperceptible. At many points there is a mighty eruption of creative energy. We must not conceive of the creative process deistically, as though God simply originated it and then left it to develop itself. Nor does He, as theistic evolution suggests, simply intervene at the point of the creation of basic categories — for instance, the great biological phyla or families. On the contrary the genetic code of each life-form is God's personal (although mediate) creation. We may adapt language used by

Paul in a different connection and say that to each form of existence God has given a body as it pleased Him. To every galaxy and every star, to each species, to every element, to each single molecule, atom, electron, proton and neutron, God has given its own being, its own character and its own destiny. Without Him, nothing came into being.

There is another principle, however, discernible in the operation of God's power in creation as well as the principle of progression. It is the principle of differentiation. The original divine fiat mentioned in Genesis 1:1 resulted in a universe without form. It was what Francis Schaeffer calls, 'Bare being' (*Genesis In Space And Time*, Hodder and Stoughton, London, 1972, p. 34). It is by a process of dividing and separating that God brings it to its ultimate condition, which He can describe as 'very good ' (Genesis 1: 31). God *divides* the light from the darkness (1:4). He *divides* the waters (vapours) of the atmosphere from the waters upon the face of the earth (1:7). He *separates* the dry land from the sea (1:9). He *divides* the day from the night (1:14).

The process of differentiation culminates in the creation of man. The momentousness of this event as a new departure is clearly highlighted in the narrative. The creation of man is preceded by God's taking counsel: 'And God said, Let us make man'. The man himself is created in the image and likeness of God and he is given dominion over all the earth and over every other life-form. This emphasis on the uniqueness of man is, of course, to be carefully qualified, not only in deference to the conclusions of modern science, but in deference also to the biblical narrative itself. Man is created on the sixth day, with the beasts of the earth and the cattle and the reptiles. Moreover, his body is formed of the dust of the ground. These facts emphasise very firmly man's affinities with lower orders of creation. His body is composed of pre-existing materials and has very close chemical affinities not only with the bodies of other animals, but with the very soil itself. Similarly, it has many anatomical and physiological features in common with various members of the animal kingdom. Yet the man is a new thing, not explicable in terms of anything that has gone before. He is no more an ape because of his anatomy than he is a dog or a pig because of his physiology or a clod of earth because of his chemistry. Even his body does not simply evolve. God creates it and in doing so repeats some of the features of the soil, the ape, the dog and the pig. And in the determination to create after His own image He breathes into the man rationality, memory, freedom of choice, a sense of beauty, longing for the fellowship of God and the distinction of self-awareness. 'Man is only a reed,' wrote Pascal, 'the weakest in nature, but he is a thinking reed. There is no need for the whole universe to take up arms to crush him: a vapour, a drop of water, is enough to kill him. But even if the universe were to crush him, man would still be nobler than his slayer, because he knows that he is dying and the advantage the universe has over him. The universe knows none of this. Thus all our dignity consists in thought' (*Pensees*, Penguin, 1966, p. 95).

The doctrine of creation is a matter of faith. 'Through faith,' says the Writer to the Hebrews, 'we understand that the worlds were framed by the word of God, so that things which are seen were not made of things which do appear' (Hebrews 11: 3). This does not mean that every detail in the process by which the universe and its various life-forms came into being is obscure to us. Many of them are accessible to us, for example, in the fossil record. The precise point which is a matter of faith is that visible things were originated by invisible, or, even more precisely, that the originated, creative force was the word of God. That word and its operations are invisible. No microscope or telescope can observe it, no balance can weigh it, no mathematical formula can define or analyse it. It is not within the reach of scientific method because it is inaccessible to our senses. The temptation facing science is to give way to its sense of frustration and impatience with (from its point of view) something so elusive, and boldly claim that it cannot exist because it is not amenable to scientific (sensory) verification. But it is unmitigated arrogance to claim that no reality can exist except that which our senses can perceive and our instruments measure. Faith understands that the world exists because of the unlimited potency of the utterance of God.

Faith does not here indicate a different degree of certainty, as if knowledge meant strong conviction and faith something more hesitant. On the contrary, faith may indicate a frame of mind where an opinion is adhered to with the utmost doggedness and tenacity. The Christian belief in creation may be, and very often is, of this kind. It may be an utterly primary conviction, held with the most cordial assurance. But it is nonetheless faith, because its basis of certainty is different from that of the scientist. We do not believe that God spoke the world into being because we have empirically verified that theory. We believe it on the testimony of God. In His Word He assures us that it is so. To put it otherwise: belief in creation by the word of God is part of the tribute we owe to Christ. It was what He believed: and our every thought is captive to the obedience of Christ. On the other hand, although the hypothesis of such a creation has never been formed independently of Scripture, yet, once formed on the authority of Christ, it may receive confirmation from the phenomena in the world around us. Certainly, none of the ascertained facts contradict the doctrine, and much of our environment becomes more intelligible in the light of it.

According to the Apostles' Creed, God the Almighty Father is the Maker of heaven and earth. But the Genesis narrative also draws attention to the creative work of the Holy Spirit: 'the Spirit of God moved on the face of the waters' (Genesis 1: 2). Even more urgently Scripture insists on the creative power of the Second Person of the Trinity, the eternal Word. 'All things were made by him,' wrote John, 'and without him was not anything made' (John 1: 3). A passage like this (and there are many others) clearly conceives of Christ as the Creator of the universe, fulfilling a cosmogenic function. But He is not only an agent in creation. He is also the first-principle (the *ARCHE*) of creation *and* the One in whom it consists or coheres *and* the One *for* whom it is. We must be careful not to speculate or even to over-interpret at this point. But it is clear that the cosmos is an expression of the personality of Christ as the wisdom of God; and that there is a union between Christ and His creation analogous to that between Him and His church. It is *in* Christ that creation is very good (Genesis 1:31) and indeed it is *in* Him that no creature (nothing created) is to be despised but to be received with thanksgiving (1 Timothy 4:4). For the same reason, the word spoken in creation (natural revelation) cannot contradict the word spoken ultimately in the incarnate Christ. Creation, being in Christ, is a free and sovereign act of God. It has in Christ a common basis with redemption and, in the event of the Fall, is subordinated to the divine purpose of grace.

The number of possible alternatives to the biblical doctrine that all that is came into being by the power of God is very limited. The essence of the Christian doctrine appears in the opening words of Genesis, 'In the beginning, God...' Before creation, God alone existed and His existence is the reason for the coming into being of all else.

The first possible alternative to this is that before creation *nothing* existed — absolutely nothing: not God, not matter, not mass, not energy, not potential, not a protoplasm, but nothing. It needs, to say the least, a fair measure of credulity to rest in this. *Ex nihilo nihil fit.* The fact that something *now* exists drives us to the conclusion that something always existed.

The second possibility is that before the creation of the universe an impersonal something existed — some protoplasm or primary particle in which all the potentialities later realised in the universe were latent. Surely, however, the existence of such an impersonal something is no less of a mystery and no less of a stumbling-block to the radically sceptical intellect than the existence of God Himself. Such a something already possesses some of the characteristics of deity, being eternal, self-existent and omnipotent. Moreover, this theory of origins is burdened with all the difficulties that face consistent materialism. The nature of the universe itself is against it. It is difficult to believe that the complexity of familiar life-forms is the result of unprogrammed molecular and genetic change; and even more difficult to convince ourselves that *Paradise Lost, Hamlet* and the *Sermon on the Mount* are derived through an inexorable sequence of cause and effect from a primitive protein.

This is not the place to pursue this theme. But the impression has got abroad not only that the Christian doctrine of the creation has been disproved but that scholars have agreed on an alternative. Neither of these assumptions is correct. There is no agreed alternative to the Christian position. Those which are affirmed are beset with enormous difficulties. The Christian doctrine, on the other hand, seems to have no peculiar difficulty of its own, is supported by a great body of argument, philosophical and scientific, and is confirmed by the whole process of special revelation in which God both asserts and describes Himself.

Power in Providence

The exhibition of God's power is not, however, limited to the work of creation. It appears equally in providence. God does not simply give the universe being. He maintains it in being, 'preserving and governing all His creatures and all their actions' (Shorter Catechism, Answer 11). Scripture testifies to this repeatedly. The Psalmist declares, 'Thou openest thine hand and satisfiest the desire of every living thing' (Psalm 145: 16). In his sermon to the Athenians Paul proclaimed that 'in him we live, and move, and have our being' (Acts 17: 28). But this power does not operate simply in terms of a kind of general superintendence. God preserves and governs minutely and particularly. His power lies behind the most trivial circumstances, accounting for the fall of the sparrow (Matthew 10: 29), the feeding of the birds (Matthew 6: 26), the growth of the lily (Matthew 6: 28) and the beauty of the grass (Matthew 6: 30). But it also lies behind the grandest and most stupendous occurrences in the world around us.

Scripture does not view nature as a closed system operating independently of God. All its operations are God's operations. So-called natural laws are only 'customs of God'. This does not mean that there are no second causes. Nor does it mean that God is merely a link in the chain of causes. All the second causes owe their potency to Him and the whole system is effective only because of the indwelling of His power. He removes the mountains (Job 9: 5ff). He commands the sun and it does not shine (Job 9: 7). He controls the morning and the dawn, the sea, the light, the storehouses of the snow, thunder, dew and frost, clouds and lightning (Job 38). He sustains the lion, the mountain-goat, the wild ass and ox, the ostrich, horse, hawk and eagle (Job 39). He commands the sea (Job 38), reigns over its raging (Psalm 65), dries it up by His rebuke (Isaiah 50: 2), calls for its waters and pours them out upon the earth (Amos 5: 8). There is the curious fact, too, that Scripture seldom says, *It rains*. Instead, *God causes it to rain*. He gives the Israelites their rains in their seasons (Leviticus 26: 4). He sends waters upon the fields (Job 5: 10), visits the earth and waters it (Psalm 65: 9) and sends rain on the righteous and on the unrighteous (Matthew 5: 45).

In sum, what we have grown accustomed to speaking of as natural forces are described by Scripture as acts of God. This is not to outlaw scientific descriptions of these occurrences or even to minimise their importance. But we must always remember that no force in the universe exists independently of God. Every process is set up by Him and sustained by Him.

The world we live in is subject to constant change. The galaxies are never at rest. The various chemical elements react endlessly with one another. The surface of the earth is subjected to the continuous processes of erosion, sedimentation, intrusion and eruption. The cells which compose living organisms are never still. The most basic particles of mass and energy, protons and neutrons, are endlessly restless. We live not in a static universe but in a world of awe-inspiring movement, collision and explosion. But every such change is rooted in the will of God and is an expression of His power. Nor are we to see Him only in the gaps — at those points where scientific explanation fails. He has set in motion the whole process which science describes. He has forged every link in the chain. He controls its every development. He is the source of all its energy.

In addition to the preservation and government of all His creatures God's providential ordering of the world also includes His restraining of the forces of evil. Here again His power is evident. Satan, the supreme evil, is a creature and all his operations are bounded by the divine will. We see this very clearly in such a passage as Job 1: 12: 'And the Lord said unto Satan, Behold, all that he has is in thy power; only upon himself put not forth thine hand. So Satan went forth from the presence of the Lord'. The New Testament carries this idea even further. Christ has destroyed the one who had the power of death (Hebrews 2: 14). He has triumphed over the forces of evil and put them to an open shame (Colossians 2:15). He has bound the strong man, the Serpent, and is now reaping the fruits of that triumph as He goes forth conquering and to conquer (Matthew 12: 29, Revelation 20: 2, Revelation 6: 2). Satan is thus bound not only by the fact of the unchallengeable supremacy of God but also by the redemptive act of Jesus Christ. In the universe, as in the Christian soul, grace reigns (Romans 5: 21) because Christ has redeemed it to God by His blood. The Lamb, not Satan, has conquered, has been found worthy to open the seals and now stands in the very midst of the throne (Revelation 5: 6). The roaring lion, wily, implacable and ubiquitous is by no means to be underestimated. But he is chained.

Power in Consummation

The final proof that creation is entirely at God's disposal is that in His own time He will bring it to an end. The power that created the aggregate of cosmic forces and sustains them in being will one day eliminate them. The present heavens and earth are kept in being by the word of God, but, as Peter reminds us, they are being reserved for judgment (2 Peter 3: 7). When that moment comes the elements will melt with fervent heat, the earth and its works will be destroyed and the heavens will pass away with a great noise. The universe as we know it will be dissolved. But there is a great prospect beyond that: 'We, according to his promise, look for new heavens and a new earth, wherein dwelleth righteousness' (2 Peter 3: 13).

Scripture gives only vague hints as to what this newness is to consist of.

For example, our Lord refers to the end as a time of regeneration: 'In the regeneration (*PALINGENESIS*) when the Son of Man shall sit on the throne of his glory, ye also shall sit upon twelve thrones, judging the twelve tribes of Israel' (Matthew 19: 28). This suggests that there is an analogy between the transformation undergone by the soul in regeneration and the change effected in the cosmos at the Consummation. The man who has been born again is a new man, yet he retains his identity and even some characteristic features of his pre-Christian past. In all probability the same will be true of the new cosmos, transformed, yet retaining its identity and many of its current features.

The same conclusion is indicated by the analogy suggested in Philippians 3: 21 between the new creation and the resurrection of the body: God will change the body of our humiliation according to the power by which He is able to subdue all things. The resurrection furnishes the believer with a new body, powerful, incorruptible, glorious and spiritual (1 Corinthians 15: 42ff). Yet in essential respects it is identical with that body which was weak and fleshly. There is every likelihood that the cosmos, too, will retain its present identity notwithstanding the grandeur of its final transformation.

The language used by Paul in 1 Corinthians 7: 31 is certainly consistent with this conclusion, if it does not indeed require it: 'The fashion (*SCHEMA*) of this world passes away'. It is the fashion, the outward appearance, of the cosmos that is to pass away, not its form or its essential nature. Like the regenerate man and the resurrection body and even the transfigured Christ the universe will undergo such a change as will transform its appearance and alter many of its most familiar features: but it will remain essentially the same.

If we ask, What is involved in this change of *SCHEMA*, there is both a negative and a positive answer.

First, God will deliver the world from its bondage to corruption (Romans 8: 21). The whole creation is involved in the curse consequent upon man's sin (Genesis 3: 17). In the consummation that curse is lifted and all the forces of evil are destroyed. The ungodly shall be no more (Psalm 104: 35). Death and hades and Satan are cast into the lake of fire (Revelation 20: 10, 14). This does not mean that they are annihilated. But they are outside. According to Matthew 8: 12, the place of weeping and gnashing of teeth is in outer darkness; and according to Revelation 22:15, sorcerers and whoremongers and murderers and idolators are again outside. Both these passages (and others) strongly suggest that all that is ungodly is located at last outside the new cosmos. Evil exists eternally, but outside. This is the final theodicy. God at the end by an act of power conquers evil, so that for the universe, as for the individual Christian, although weeping endures for the night, joy comes with the morning (Psalm 30: 5).

Secondly, and positively, the final regeneration brings about a cosmos which is new in the sense that only righteousness dwells within it. The present state of the world is determined by the unrighteousness of the first Adam. Its final state will be determined by the righteousness of Christ, the last Adam. It will be glorious and blessed in Him. It will become the inheritance of the meek (Matthew 5: 5) and will be perfectly adapted to their needs. It will occasion them no tears, subject them to no discomfort and frustrate none of their aspirations (Revelation 7: 16f). It will be resplendent with the glory of their Saviour: 'The glory of God did lighten it, and the Lamb is the light thereof' (Revelation 21: 23). And its every beauty, comfort and provision will be theirs.

Our confidence that this is the pattern of our future rests solely on the promise of God (2 Peter 3: 13). There are no evidences in the world around us that such a consummation is either imminent or inevitable. Nor do we know of any force within the universe capable of effecting it. What we do know is that the God who made this world and who at present sustains it has declared His intention to transform it, and although our minds may stagger at the magnitude of the undertaking, yet, in the face of His almightiness, such hesitation is absurd. Here, too, what He has promised, He is able to perform (Rom. 4: 21).

The Power of God in Redemption

There is the closest possible connection between providence and redemption, basically because God's intention to save lies at the very heart of His preservation of the world, His restraining of evil and the final act of consummation. The position of Christ in the cosmos is the guarantee of this. He is in the midst of the throne, as the Lamb who has been slain (Revelation 5: 6). He opens the seals of God's purpose in His capacity as Redeemer (Revelation 5: 9). He is the head over all things for the church (Ephesians 1: 22). It is God's purpose to gather up all things in Him (Ephesians 1: 10). He has authority over all flesh precisely in order to give eternal life to all those whom the Father has given Him (John 17: 2). All these passages make clear that the Redeemer is sovereign over the whole of history and that He regulates it precisely in the interests of redemption. He moves heaven and earth as the One who 'loved me and gave himself for me' (Galatians 2: 20).

It is only in the interests of clarity, therefore, that one may treat of God's power in redemption as distinct from His power in providence. In reality, these are not separate. Providence is redemptive through and through: 'God works all things together for the good of those who love Him' (Romans 8: 28).

The power of God in redemption appears, first of all, in connection with the creation of the human nature of our Lord: 'The Holy Spirit shall come upon you, and the *power* of the Highest shall overshadow you: therefore also that holy thing which shall be born of you shall be called the Son of God' (Luke 1: 35). The humanity of Christ was called into being by an utterly supernatural act of God. Jesus Christ is not a development from within human history, to be explained from what has gone before. He is an intrusion into history, an utterly new force come to effect a new beginning. He was born, to quote an interesting variant on the text of John 1: 13, not by the will of the flesh, nor by the will of a man, but of God. We must remember, however, that although His manhood was supernaturally originated it was in itself essentially the same as ours. The development of the foetus and the birth of the child were perfectly normal. Moreover, the constitution of His human nature was exactly the same as ours, sin excepted. He had a true human body and a reasonable soul. He was of the Virgin's substance, in the sense that she contributed to Him what any human mother contributes to her child. He was born with all the essential properties and all the common infirmities of men. And the pattern of dependence upon the Father and the Spirit established at His conception continued throughout His entire ministry. He had to be upheld (Isaiah 42: 1), He had to exercise trust (Hebrews 12: 2), He had to be comforted. He had to pray and He had to have the assurance that the Father was with Him. Indeed, it was through the eternal Spirit that He at last offered Himself without spot to God (Hebrews 9: 14).

The same power is put forth again to effect the resurrection of Christ. Significantly, this act is referred to each of the three persons of the Godhead. It is ascribed to God the Father, who loosed the bands of death (Acts 2: 24), raised Him from the dead (Galatians 1:1) and begat the church again to a living hope by the resurrection (1 Peter 1: 3). It is also ascribed to Christ Himself. It was not possible that He, who is the resurrection and the life, should be held by death. He had power to resume His own life (John 10: 18). He would rebuild the temple of His body (John 2: 21). The Spirit's agency in the resurrection is not so clearly asserted, but it seems to be implied in two passages in the Epistle to the Romans. It was according to the Spirit of holiness that He was declared the Son of God by the resurrection from the dead (Romans 1: 4); and, it is to the Spirit of Him who raised up Jesus from the dead that we look for the resurrecting of our own mortal bodies (Romans 8: 11).

Like the virgin-birth the resurrection is portrayed in the New Testament as a completely supernatural act for which the power of God is the only explanation. Underlying this, however, is the further emphasis that the resurrection is the appropriate reward for the Son's obedience. He is glorified because He finished the work given Him to do, and highly exalted because He was obedient unto death. He had contracted sin and become liable to death by becoming the substitute of His people. Having died, however, He is discharged of that debt: 'Death has no more dominion over Him' (Romans 6: 9). The resurrection is a declaration of both His own and His people's immunity; and beyond that, it is the seal of God's approval. The word spoken in anticipation at both the Baptism and the Transfiguration is now magnificently underlined: 'This is my beloved Son, in whom I am well pleased' (Mark 1: 11, Matthew 17: 5).

The power of God appears equally in the application of redemption. The regeneration of the soul is ascribed to the same cause as the regeneration of the world. We were born again by the word of God (1 Peter 1: 23). Paul again sees the new birth as analogous to fiat-creation: 'God who commanded the light to shine out of darkness has shined in our hearts' (2 Corinthians 4: 6). The result of this experience is described, therefore, as a new creation (2 Corinthians 5: 17). The power of God has reached into the depths of our hearts in spiritual renewal, transforming the well-springs of thought and action. The product is a 'new man' (Colossians 3: 10), changed in every faculty of his soul. He sees where formerly he was blind. He is strong where formerly he was weak. He is free where formerly he was bound.

This change is definitive and irreversible. It is also, however, the base from which we move forward in progressive sanctification. We can grow into conformity to the image of God's Son only if first of all we have been quickened by the Spirit of God. In this growth and development we ourselves have an indispensable part to play, working out our own salvation (Philippians 2: 12) and purifying ourselves as God is pure (1 John 3:3). Yet here again there is an operation of God's power. He conforms us to the image of His Son (Romans 8: 29). It is by the Spirit of the Lord that we are transformed (2 Corinthians 3: 18). It is the Father who sanctifies by the truth (John 17: 17) and by the Spirit that the deeds of the body are mortified (Romans 8: 13). Similarly, it is the God who initiates and sustains this growth who at last consummates it. The One who predestinates, glorifies (Romans 8: 30).

In regeneration and sanctification, of course, God's power operates through the Word (1 Peter 1: 23; 2: 2). The Word by itself, however, has no efficacy. It may be an authentic Word proclaimed in all sincerity, clarity and earnestness by a God-sent preacher, and yet fall on stony ground (Mark 4:16). Men's minds are naturally closed against the truth (Acts 16: 14) and blind to the glory and relevance of Christ (1 Corinthians 2: 14). Humanly speaking, these barriers are impenetrable, and the whole hope of the witnessing church lies in the fact that God has promised power precisely in connection with preaching the gospel (Acts 1: 8). Thus the message comes not in word only, but in power (1 Thessalonians 1: 5): men's hearts are opened (Acts 16: 14) and they receive the things of the Spirit of God (1 Corinthians 2: 12). The change effected by God's power at this point is not, however, in the message itself, nor in the preacher, but in the hearer. Grace makes him responsive and sensitive to the Word so that, convinced of its truth and pricked in his heart, he receives it gladly (Acts 2:41).

The power of God is demonstrated equally in the preservation of the believer. He is kept by the power of God through faith (1 Peter 1:5). He is inherently vulnerable, weak and inconsistent — no match for the gates of hell and the wiles of the devil. The world is organised to wage war on his faith through its scholarship, its religion and its political might. On the face of it, there is every likelihood that his faith will fail. But God keeps him: as a garrison within him (1 Peter 1: 5), a sentry at the door of his heart (Philippians 4: 7), an army around him (Psalm 34: 7) and a support beneath him (Deuteronomy 33: 27). The believer will never perish, because no power can pluck him from the Father's hand (John 10: 28, 29) or separate him from His love (Romans 8: 39). God will perfect the work of salvation which He has begun (Philippians 1: 6).

We never outgrow this need to be kept. It must continue 'unto salvation'. No point can be reached on this side of glory at which the believer may imagine that he can now safely continue on his own. The mature (even those on the threshold of the world to come) need it no less than the novice. Furthermore, sometimes this preservation is effected by God's acting as a restraining force upon the Christian himself. This is clearly recognised in such a passage as Psalm 19: 13: 'Keep back your servant from presumptuous sin.' Often it needs all the strength of God Himself to hold us back from high-handed sin.

Yet this power does not keep us as automata. We are not inert and passive objects in the hands of God. We must follow the Shepherd. We must put on the whole armour of God. We must patiently endure hardship. Above all, we must have faith in the power of God (1 Peter 1: 5). Even when we walk in darkness, we must trust in the name of the Lord and, knowing our own infirmities, earnestly implore His protection.

A particular aspect of God's keeping us is that He affords the Christian constant support in times of stress and need. This is clearly exemplified in the experience of Paul. He was burdened with the care of all the churches. He was opposed by false prophets and by the leaders of various factions. He was buffeted by Satan. He was persecuted by both the Jewish and the Imperial powers. He was constantly on the move facing the fatigue and discomfort and danger which that involved. Yet he found that he was constantly renewed (2 Corinthians 4: 16), that God's grace was sufficient for him (2 Corinthians 12:9), that he could do all things through Christ strengthening him (Philippians 4:13) and that with every temptation God provided a way of escape (1 Corinthians 10:13). The Old Testament emphasises the same point. Even where young men faint and become weary and utterly fail, those who wait on the Lord renew their strength; they run and do not weary and walk and do not faint (Isaiah 40: 30f). There is nothing greater in the life of the church than to see men and women, temperamentally and constitutionally weak and fragile, enabled to endure what would make strong men quake: able to be patient in affliction, content whatever their circumstances, and making melody in their hearts always and in all things (Ephesians 5:20). That is the acme of Christian achievement and one of the most moving accomplishments of omnipotence.

The redemptive operation of God's power culminates in His raising believers from the dead. This is a direct and immediate act of the risen and sovereign Christ who will change the bodies of our humiliation and conform them to the body of His own glory (Philippians 3: 21). Scripture is fully aware of the apparent absurdity of the doctrine, but it resolutely insists that the deed lies easily within the compass of the divine power just as it asserts that that power is the only, and yet the totally adequate, basis of our hope. He will give to each a body as it pleases Him (1 Corinthians 15: 38) and He will do so simply because He is able to subdue all things to Himself (Philippians 3: 21). In the face of death we are sustained by the faith of Abraham, who yielded his only son to God in the confidence that He was able to raise him up, even from the dead (Hebrews 11: 19).

Divine power and religious experience

The power of God is closely connected with some of our most basic religious experiences. For one thing, it is obviously part of that intimidatingness of God which calls forth the most elementary of all our religious attitudes: the fear of God. It is the perception of this overwhelming power which caused Isaiah to say 'Woe is me! for I am undone' (Isaiah 6: 5). God is able to sweep us to desolation in a moment (Psalm 73: 19) and to break us in pieces like a potter's sherd (Psalm 2: 9).

It is surprising, however, how often Scripture directs us to God's power for our *comfort*. It is because He never faints or becomes weary that we can hope to mount up on wings as eagles (Isaiah 40: 31). The works of the Lord inspire confidence in those who have turned to Him as their refuge (Psalm 46: 8). When we ask whence our help comes we rejoice in the knowledge that our safety is from the Lord who made heaven and earth (Psalm 121: 2). Elisha can be fearless because the forces that are with him are greater than those that are against him (2 Kings 6: 16).

The same emphasis is found in the New Testament. The power (*DUNAMIS*) of God means that no man is able (*DUNATAI*) to pluck us from the Father's hand nor any creature able to separate us from His love (John 10: 29, Romans 8: 39). Against hope we may believe in hope, because God is able to perform what He has promised (Romans 4: 21). As we face all the difficulties, stumbling-blocks and pit-falls of the Christian way we are upheld by the knowledge that God is able to keep us from falling and to present us faultless before the presence of His glory with exceeding joy (Jude 24). When we are buffeted by Satan our comfort is that God's strength is made perfect in our weakness (2 Corinthians 12: 9). Things which would ordinarily fill men with bitterness we can endure with contentment because we can do all things through Christ strengthening us.

Finally, it is the power of God that gives the church confidence as it faces its missionary task: 'you shall receive power, after the Holy Spirit comes on you, and you shall be witnesses to me' (Acts 1: 8). As a rushing mighty wind that power is resident in the church, rests upon each of its members and courses through its ministry so that at last the foolishness of preaching becomes the power of God unto salvation.

The Hiding of His Power?

How fully do God's works reveal His power? His power is at least great enough to create the universe; great enough to sustain it in being; and great enough to account for the aggregate of forces within it. But God has a power beyond what is expressed in His works. He can do infinitely more than He has done and will do. This is well illustrated in the third chapter of Habakkuk, with its description of the mighty operation of God's power on Mount Sinai at the beginning of Israel's history. Then God measured the earth; He drove asunder the nations; He scattered the everlasting mountains; He caused the hills to sink low; He split the earth with rivers; He caused the sun and moon to stand still; He marched through the earth in indignation, trampling the heathen and smashing the heads of the wicked. The recollection made the prophet tremble. And yet, it was only *the hiding of His power* (Habakkuk 3:4). It was not an exhaustive demonstration. For all its brilliance, it was only a dim shadow of the reality. It disclosed no more of the greatness of divine power than the vision of Isaiah Six did of the glory of His holiness. We are given enough light to realise that if these hints or suggestions are so overwhelming how much more so the hidden power itself! But never enough to imagine that there is no more beyond.

CHAPTER FIVE

GOD'S MIGHTY ACTS

God's power is manifest, as we have seen, in the works of creation, providence and redemption. It appears with special clarity, however, in the category of events referred to by Scripture as 'miracles'. These are not additional to God's works of redemptive providence, but they are distinct enough to deserve special attention. Scripture applies to them three particular designations. First, they are wonders (*TERATA*). This word defines them by way of their emotional impact upon those who witnessed them. They were filled with amazement, because these events were utterly extraordinary and completely different from anything with which past experience had made them familiar. Secondly, the miracles were signs (*SEMEIA*). They were tokens of God's presence and of His approval and commissioning of those who performed them. They were marks of the special status of our Lord Himself and of His prophets and apostles. They were proofs that His kingdom had come. They were encouragements and inducements to steadfastness and endeavour.

Thirdly, and above all, they were mighty acts (*DUNAMEIS*). They were effects of the power of God, His dynamic intervention in the plight of man. They were commensurate with His power. They were explicable only in terms of His power.

Events of this kind occurred throughout the history of redemption. Nevertheless, they were more characteristic of some periods than of others. They mark, first of all, the period of the Exodus, that great, typical redemption of the Old Testament and the moment of the inauguration of the nation, Israel. They became abundant again in the ministries of Elijah and Elisha, to authenticate the great prophetic movement of which these men were the first representatives. And, of course, they were characteristic features of the ministry of our Lord, who healed the sick, cast out demons, rebuked the elements and raised the dead. These were the signs of the Messiah, God the Father's witness to His glory and the seal of His approval (Acts 2: 22).

It is easy enough to give a list of these events referred to by Scripture as miracles. It is much more difficult to give a definition. It is not enough to say that they are works which are either contrary to nature or above nature, because nature is not a biblical concept and its use is an obstacle to proper Christian insight.[1] We must fall back on the biblical terminology itself. The miracle must be a *wonder*, an event occurring in the objective, phenomenal universe, which fills people with a sense of amazement because it belongs to an utterly unfamiliar order of reality. Secondly, it must be a *sign*. It must be attestative of the person performing it, or interpretative of the nature of his work or indicative of the imminent fulfilment of God's promises. Thirdly, it must be an act of the divine *might*. God has created this universe. He determines the order according to which its events occur. He is not confronted with some unalterable causal nexus or a closed system of natural laws, but with a universe which is utterly open to Him, pervaded by Him and totally plastic in His hands. What we call its laws are only descriptions of the way that God usually preserves and governs particular segments of it. Indeed, man himself, made in the image of God, is easily able to interfere in its operations and does so frequently. As an intelligent agent, he is able to change the direction of its forces, to restrain them and to harness them. He can precipitate almost endless reactions between its various elements.

The operation of God in miracle is analogous to this. He is free and able to interfere. Scripture speaks of 'the finger of God'(Luke 11: 20). Browning speaks of 'a flash of the will that can'. God may suspend certain normal relationships and sequences within the creation. He may intrude, as in *fiat* creation, and say, 'Let there be!' There is no violation of the laws of nature, because there is no nature. The miracle is a new event. But it is perfectly intelligible because of the presence of a new and adequate cause, the power of God. Sometimes this means that an event is not followed by what normally follows it: for example, the death of Christ is not followed by the putrefaction of His body. At other times, a comparatively trivial event is followed by another which is utterly spectacular: some spittle applied to the eye restores sight to the blind, or a word is spoken and the dead rise. In these instances, the effect produced is altogether disproportionate to the apparent energy put

[1]The term nature, is of course, ambivalent. It is sometimes used with the meaning *inborn mind, character, instinct or disposition*. In this sense the term *is* found in Scripture (e.g. Rom. 1: 26, Rom. 2: 14, 1 Cor. 11: 14). Since the eighteenth century, however, scientists (and poets) have tended to use the word in another sense, *viz., the power that creates and regulates the world*. Here Nature is a God-substitute. It is this latter use of the term which is un-biblical.

forth. On yet other occasions, an event occurs without any precedent which might serve as an explanation. The outstanding example of this is the resurrection of Christ. In all these different forms of miracle the new event is explained by the intrusion of a new cause, the finger of God.

We must not, however, take this to mean that the power of God operates only in miracle. He has created the whole system of cause and effect and He sustains and directs it. Every particle of mass and energy has exactly the character which He has imparted to it and behaves exactly as He directs. But in miracle God does something unusual, so that the might of His power becomes evident to the amazement of men, and they are driven to ask, What does this mean?

The major obstacle to belief in miracles is the prevalence of an unbiblical and un-scientific concept of nature. We have fallen into the habit of speaking of it anthropomorphically, as if it were an agent in its own right, possessing an independent intelligence, gifted with marvellous foresight and capable of choosing and pursuing its own objectives. Darwin, for example, can write: 'Natural selection picks out with unerring skill the best varieties' (Quoted in Hooykaas *Religion and the Rise of Modern Science*, Edinburgh, 1973, p. 18; I have not been able to find this precise wording in Darwin himself). Such personification may have some justification in poetry. In scientific description it is misleading nonsense. Natural selection has no skill, because natural selection does not exist, any more than nature exists. These are only logical categories. The same applies to the phrase, 'laws of nature'. There are no such laws. There are only customs of God, describing the way that He normally preserves and governs the world of created reality, in all its fulness and variety. That world is constantly changing and man, observing these changes, can detect patterns and predict new formations. But every such change is rooted in divine decision. The will of God is the ultimate reality, governing the behaviour of atoms and galaxies, genes and protons. That world cannot exclude God from His creation. The sequence of change has no power to insist that God shall never alter it. He may at any point, for good reason, depart from His own custom and cause any force or element to behave in an utterly new way.

Another difficulty is that man, faced with the fact of miracle, is blinded by rationalism. We are accustomed to a certain pattern of occurrences, and this creates the prejudice that any departure from this order is impossible. Nothing is deemed real which contradicts this prejudice. In the past, this has wrought havoc with scientific investigation. Facts had to be accommodated to the prejudice that the earth was flat; that this planet was the centre of the universe; that the motion of all stars was circular; that there could be no fissure of the atom. The effect of such an attitude was to relegate observation and experimentation to a secondary role. Theory took precedence over fact, and rationalistic commitment to a certain view of reality prevented the evidence, however cogent, from getting a hearing.

The prevalence of this mentality is the real reason for the outright rejection of the miraculous. We have an *a priori* commitment to the theory that miracles do not happen. The dead do not rise. A mere word does not still a storm. This attitude finds its classic expression in the statement of Goethe: 'A voice from heaven would not convince me that water burned or a dead man rose again' (Quoted in Warfield, *op. cit.* p. 195). This surely is pure prejudice. We have made our generalisation before investigating the facts: and it is such a generalisation as precludes our looking at the facts. This is inadmissible.

The only scientific attitude is enshrined in the words of Huxley: 'We must sit down before the facts as little children' (Hooykaas, *Religion and the Rise of Modern Science*, p. 51). It is a fact that the tomb of Christ was empty; that He was seen after His death by many witnesses of different temperaments and under different circumstances; that the interpretation put upon their experiences by these witnesses was that He had risen; that their own lives and the history of the world were transformed by their belief; and that they were prepared to lay down their lives for their faith. This evidence may at the end of the day lack cogency. But it deserves better than to be dismissed because it will not fit into our prejudiced view of what is possible. At last, the principle that miracles did not occur because they could not occur will have to yield to the fact that they can occur because they did occur. The evidence we have is not evidence to their miraculousness. It is simply evidence to their factuality. The tomb was empty. Christ was seen. To say that these things are impossible is to be blinded by unscientific rationalism.

'There are more things in heaven
and earth, Horatio,
Then are dreamt of in your
philosophy.'
(*Hamlet*, Act I Sc 5)

Why, however, did God not create the universe so as to avoid the need for these corrective and remedial interferences? To some extent, this objection rests on a misunderstanding. The universe is not static. It is characterised by constant movement. This is true both of its greatest masses and of its tiniest particles; and all these movements are rooted in the will of God. The cosmos moves and has its being in Him. Miracles must not be seen, therefore, as isolated instances of movement and change in an otherwise immobile universe. At the same time, however, miracles represent unusual and extraordinary change. They are departures from the norm. The necessity for such departures arises from the fact that the universe (as seen in Christian revelation) is in an abnormal condition. The fall of man into sin has led to cosmic derangement. The ground is cursed. Creation is in bondage to vanity, and groans and travails (Romans 8: 22). The time is out of joint. Hence the need for God's restorative and curative intervention in redemption and for the miracles as integral parts of that redemption. The plight of man calls for these extraordinary intrusions of divine power. We should also note that the nature of the miracles harmonises completely with the nature of redemption. They are appropriate to the nature of the problem; they are congruous with the nature of God; and above all they fit perfectly into the context of the Saviour's person and work. Had He come with no hint of supernaturalism, *that* would have been deemed incredible. Now that He has come attested by miracles, wonders and signs, these very attestations are alleged as objections against Him. What eloquent confirmation that the mind of man is enmity against God! It was surely perfectly fitting that the Son of God should heal the sick, cast out devils, still the waves and raise the dead: and quite incredible that He should enter history without causing a ripple.

CHAPTER SIX

THE PRESENCE OF GOD

The most eloquent statement of God's omnipresence is in Psalm 139, where the psalmist speaks of himself as beset by God: 'Thou hast beset me behind and before, and laid thine hand upon me' (verse 5). There is no privacy. Nor is there any possibility of flight. Should he go to the outermost bounds of the universe, God is there. Should he make his bed in Sheol, 'Thou there!' Should he go to some remote corner of the earth, moving with the speed of light, 'even there shall thy hand lead me and thy right hand shall hold me' (verse 10). Even as a foetus in his mother's womb he was utterly open to the scrutiny of God. It is no wonder that he cries in anguish, 'Whither shall I go from thy spirit? or whither shall I flee from thy presence?' (verse 7). Everywhere there is God; His being, His revelation, His sovereignty and His scrutiny. He is inescapable: and so is our consciousness of Him and our awareness of our own dependence and accountability. A creature is localised. When it is here it is not there and when it is there it is not here. Not so God. He is fully present simultaneously at every point in His creation. He is both here and there in the fulness of His being, attributes, functions and prerogatives, upholding all things, revealing Himself through all things and impinging on the consciousness of every rational creature.

Present to the Church Triumphant

One implication of this is that in the absolute sense there is no place where God is nearer than He is at another. Yet Scripture makes plain that in an evangelical sense God may be both notably near us and notably far from us. The church triumphant enjoys His presence in a special sense. Standing before the throne of God (Revelation 7: 15) it sees not through a glass, enigmatically, but face to face. It beholds Christ as He is. This is a presence involving consummate intimacy of fellowship, unspeakable comfort and immeasurably enhanced understanding. Even the physical environment is redolent of the unqualified beneficence of God: 'They shall hunger no more, neither thirst any more; neither shall the sun shine upon them, nor any heat' (Revelation 7: 16). They enjoy the privilege of the physical nearness of incarnate God and their blessedness is closely connected with that: 'The Lamb which is in the midst of the throne shall feed them, and shall lead them to the fountain of the water of life: and God shall wipe away all tears from their eyes' (Revelation 7: 17).

The Nearness of Grace

But even in this life, there is a special nearness to God: the nearness of grace. This is particularly important at times of difficulty: 'Though I walk through the valley of the shadow of death, I will fear no evil: for thou art with me' (Psalm 23: 4). The same sentiment is expressed in Isaiah 43: 2: 'When thou passest through the waters I will be with thee.' Similar terms are used in connection with more public calamities in Psalm 46: 1,2: 'God is our refuge and strength, a very present help in trouble. Therefore will not we fear, though the earth be removed and though the mountains be carried into the midst of the sea.' Indeed, this was the distinctive privilege of the Old Testament church: 'God is in the midst of her; she shall not be moved: God shall help her and that right early' (Psalm 46: 5). This is equally true of the New Testament church. The promise of God's presence is an integral part of the Great Commission: 'Go ye, therefore, and teach all nations . . . and, lo, I am with you always, even to the end of the world' (Matthew 28: 19).

This presence means, primarily, God's help as we face the stresses of our own personal situations. We are promised grace to help us in times of need (Hebrews 4: 16), even to the extent that we shall be able to do all things in the One who strengthens us (Philippians 4: 13). This idea pervades Scripture and is set forth in terms of virtually every preposition human language has to offer. God is *with* us (Matthew 28: 20), *around* us (Psalm 34: 7), *in* us (John 14: 17), *in the midst of* us (Psalm 46: 5), *behind* us (Psalm 139: 5), *underneath* us (Deuteronomy 33: 27), *near* us (Psalm 148: 14) and *before* us (John 10: 4). The metaphors used are equally varied: God is a *shepherd*, a *captain*, an encircling *army*, an indwelling *garrison*, a *sentry* at the door, a *watchman*, even a *broody hen*.

In all these ways God stands by His people, nourishing, keeping and teaching them. Confidence in this is one of the great foundations of the Christian life. It is not something to be worked up to. It is to be presupposed, even taken for granted, as we face our individual obligations, the wiles of the Devil and what Paul calls 'the sufferings of the present time'. We share Christ's own assurance, 'I am not alone, because the Father is with me' (John 16: 32). That is not something variable, true or untrue according to our personal feelings. It is one of the constants and one of the fundamental assumptions of our Christian lives.

God's Presence Withdrawn

Scripture tells us equally clearly, however, that this gracious presence of God can sometimes be withdrawn. Isaiah speaks of Israel as separated from God (Isaiah 59: 2), as complaining that her way is hid from the Lord and as a people walking in darkness and having no light (Isaiah 40: 27; 50: 10). David speaks similarly of being forsaken (Psalm 22: 1) and describes the church as cast off (Psalm 74: 1).

What lies behind this kind of language? In the highest sense, God never forsakes the believer. He says so explicitly: 'I will not fail thee or forsake thee' (Joshua 1: 5). He is invincibly determined to save us and His love will never let go until He presents us faultless in the presence of His glory (Jude 24). Clearly, then, believers will always enjoy that presence of God which is essential to their perseverance. They will be kept right up to the completion of their salvation (1Peter 1: 5).

It is quite consistent with this, however, that some aspects of God's presence may be withdrawn. For example, there may be times when every outward indication of God's love is withheld. Wherever we look, we see only calamity. This is not itself necessarily a withdrawing of God's presence. He may be present at precisely that moment, unobtrusively supporting and guiding us. But when God also withholds all sense of His love and all ability to be patient and all understanding of His will, then, in a very real sense, we walk in darkness and have no light.

At other times the loss of the presence of God means that He withdraws the help we were accustomed to. This is well illustrated in Samson's encounter with Delilah. He rises to face the Philistines, taking the divine help for granted, only to find, to his dismay, that it is no longer there. Similarly, ignorant of the sin of Achan, Joshua sends three thousand men to capture Ai, confident of God's help, only to experience ignominious defeat (Joshua 7: 1ff.). There are similar moments in our own Christian lives: times when God leaves us to defeat and failure. Responsibilities become unbearable, the Tempter wins easy victories and the very grasshopper becomes a burden. These experiences are not arbitrary, the reflection merely of some divine whim. God does not afflict willingly (Lamentations 3:

33). The true explanation lies in the words of Isaiah: 'The Lord's hand is not shortened that it cannot save. But your iniquities have separated between you and your God, and your sins have hid his face from you, that he will not hear' (Isaiah 59: 1, 2).

At yet other times God may withdraw His presence in the sense of withholding its consolations. We may be both kept and helped and yet we ourselves, because unaware of it, derive no comfort from it. The most solemn instance of this is the experience of our Lord on the cross. He is both beloved by God and upheld by God and yet He is devoid of all comfort: 'My God, my God, why hast thou forsaken me?' (Mark 15: 34). On an infinitely lower plane, there may be moments when we ourselves enjoy the presence of God in a powerfully sustaining way and yet feel very much alone and forsaken. Sometimes this feeling of forsakenness is the result of God's Spirit being grieved and His witness muted. At other times we ourselves put up barriers against God's comfort. God loves us: and His Word, His Spirit and His providence all testify to that. Yet we fail to hear either because of lack of faith or because of persistent and even wilful melancholy and self-pity.

Even the spiritual man, then, sometimes lacks the presence of God. For the natural man, this is his day-to-day situation. It is the only relation to God he has ever known. His Creator is always at a distance, remote, inaccessible and threatening. This is graphically illustrated in Genesis 3: 24. After his act of defiance man is expelled from Eden. He must live, for ever afterwards, in estrangement from God. But that is not all. Not only is man expelled. The way back is barred. There is a flaming sword which turns every way to guard the way to the tree of life. This does not mean that there is absolutely no way back. But any attempt to end the alienation must reckon seriously with the flaming sword. Communion can only be re-established by a specific act of reconciliation. This is precisely the significance of the atonement. Christ makes peace *through the blood of His cross* (Colossians 1: 20). The flaming sword is plunged into the heart of the Last Adam (Zechariah 13: 7). Only through that vicarious curse-bearing can the problem of the inaccessibility of God be overcome.

The Presence of the Kingdom

Another distinct phase in the Bible's concept of the presence of God is provided by the idea of the coming of the Kingdom.

This is an important element in the teaching of both our Lord and John the Baptist. This kingdom was not, of course, territorial. It was the reign of God spoken of so frequently in the Old Testament. God was King. He reigned over Israel and, even more important, He reigned *for* Israel (Deuteronomy 33: 26). But alongside this assertion there was a hope: that one day the King would come to save His people and to destroy their enemies. This appears very clearly in such a passage as Psalm 96: 12f.: 'Then shall the trees of the field rejoice before Jehovah: for he cometh, for he cometh to judge the earth: he shall judge the world with righteousness and the people with his truth.' This is the innermost essence of Old Testament messianic prophecy (which is not the same as saying that it was the essence of the people's expectation). Jehovah was King and the King was going to come. That was where the Old Testament ended: 'The Lord whom ye seek shall suddenly come to his temple' (Malachi 3: 1). And this is where the New Testament begins:'Repent ye, for the kingdom of heaven is at hand' (Matthew 3: 2). The King has come.

Yet this concept of the coming of the kingdom is a complex one. Attempts have been made to interpret it exclusively in terms of a *realised* eschatology: that is, as an event which has already occurred in a complete and unrepeatable sense. Others have gone to the opposite extreme and taken it in a wholly *futurist* sense as a promise which has not yet received any kind of fulfilment. It seems very clear from the New Testament that we are not obliged to choose between these two interpretations. It is true both that the kingdom has come and that the kingdom is yet to come. There is even a third dimension: in the present, in the time between the first and second advents of our Lord, the kingdom is constantly coming.

First of all, the kingdom has come. It is at hand. C. H. Dodd, the foremost exponent of realised eschatology, laid much stress on the particular verb used in, for example, Mark 1: 15, claiming, with considerable justification that *eggiken* means 'has come' (*The Parables of The Kingdom*, Fontana 1965, p.37). But the case does not rest on this linguistic argument alone. It is supported by many wider considerations. Christ is Immanuel. In Him, God is with us. In Him, the King has come. In Him, the time is fulfilled (Mark. 1: 15). In Him, the last days are upon us (Hebrews 1: 2; 1 John 2: 18). In Him, men experience the powers of the age to come (Hebrews 6: 5). He is the redemptive assertion of God's sovereignty, the intrusion of God's grace into history. In Him, the power of God comes to grips with the plight of man. He is the glory of God, the very Shekinah itself, tabernacling among men.

The tangible physicalness of this form of the divine presence should not be overlooked. During those years men could see His glory (John 1: 14). They could witness with amazement His mighty acts. They could literally hear Him expound the ethics of His kingdom. God was on earth, experiencing the human condition at first hand and engaging the Enemy at close quarters. He was present in our poverty, our suffering and our temptations until the last moment of supreme paradox when He dwelt in the anathema. Then the Cross became His Tabernacle.

But in an equally important sense the kingdom is coming, gradually but inexorably, in the present. This is what we are taught to pray for in the Lord's Prayer: 'Thy kingdom come!" (Matthew 6: 10). It comes when the seed of the Word falls on good soil and bears fruit (Matthew 13: 8, 23), when men hear Christ's words and do them (Matthew 7: 24ff.) and when sinners go through the strait gate and begin to walk along the narrow way. Then men escape from the authority of Darkness, come under the dominion of Christ and experience the Power of the age to come.

The Presence of the Spirit

It is impossible to understand this aspect of the coming of the kingdom without reference to another distinctive strand in New Testament teaching, namely, the mission of the Comforter. Just as the coming of the kingdom in the past, realised sense is bound up inseparably with the unique form of the divine presence involved in the incarnation so the continuous present coming of the kingdom can only be understood in terms of the divine presence involved in the coming of the Holy Spirit. The church looks back to the *parousia* of Christ at Bethlehem and forward to His *parousia* at the End. But it also enjoys the *parousia* of the Lord here and now in the presence of the Holy Spirit.

This presence was inaugurated at Pentecost, when the disciples (all without exception) received the Spirit, were baptised in the Spirit and were filled with the Spirit. This was to be the norm for the new dispensation. The presence of God was to mean in practice the dwelling of the Spirit in every believer.

Some of the peculiar features of this presence are clearly hinted at in the audio-visual signs which accompanied

Pentecost.

First, the *wind*. In the Old Testament the words for *spirit* and for *wind* or *breath* are the same and what is being suggested here is that in the New Testament age the Spirit is the breath of God blowing like a rushing mighty wind through the church. The invincible energy of God has come upon her and her ministry in the world is to reflect that. The church is to be a mighty force, at once creative and destructive. It will re-make human lives: but it will also pull down the strongholds of error and ungodliness. One cannot but ask in the passing: Is this the church as we know it today? and if not, why not?

Secondly, *fire*. Throughout Scripture fire is symbolic of the purity and integrity of Jehovah. At Horeb, for example, God appears in the burning bush. Similarly at Sinai the mountain burns with fire. The fire of Acts 2. 3, therefore, is a reminder that the presence of God with the post-Pentecost church is a presence of holiness. Nor does such symbolism end with the Old Testament. It continues into the New: 'Our God is a consuming fire' (Hebrews 12: 29). It is against this background that we are to interpret the 'cloven fire-like tongues' of Acts 2: 3. The greatest privilege of the New Testament church is that it enjoys the presence of God. But this is always the presence of the holy God, of God in His integrity. In the midst of the church there is a consuming fire, the solemn, almost terrifying, character of which must always modify Christian behaviour: 'Who among us can dwell with everlasting burnings?' (Isaiah 33: 14).

This point is vividly underlined in the story of Ananias and Sapphira (Acts 5: 1-11). Their offence is directly against the Spirit of holiness and their punishment dramatically reinforces the need for scrupulously careful conduct on the part of all members of the Christian community. Precisely because God lives among us there is a special urgency in the demand, 'Be ye holy, for I am holy' (Leviticus 11: 44). The same point is brought out clearly in 2 Corinthians 6: 16ff. We are the temple of God. God dwells in us and walks among us: 'Having therefore these promises, dearly beloved, let us cleanse ourselves from all filthiness of the flesh and spirit, perfecting holiness in the fear of God.'

Thirdly, *tongues*. Cloven tongues, as if of fire, sit upon each of the believers and they all begin to speak as the Spirit gives them utterance. During His earthly ministry the Lord had related the ministry of the Comforter in the closest possible way to the mission of the church. For example, He had told the disciples, 'When the Comforter is come, he shall testify of me' (John 15: 26); and again, 'He will convict the world of sin and of righteousness and of judgment' (John 16: 8). Even more explicit was the promise recorded in Acts 1: 8: 'Ye shall receive power and ye shall be witnesses to me in Jerusalem and in all Judea and in Samaria and unto the uttermost part of the earth.' And of course the same connection is made in the Great Commission: 'Go and teach all nations; and, lo I am with you always.'

It is in harmony with these passages that the Spirit is given pre-eminently as a Spirit of tongues to a church whose primary function is to preach the gospel to Jew and Gentile, to Greek and Barbarian. Only by the Spirit's help can the church have insight into the message of Christ; only through the Spirit does it have the requisite boldness; and only through the Spirit does it possess the necessary courage to confront the world with the gospel.

It is significant, too, that the tongues fell on each of them. The work of evangelism is not to be left to any specialist preaching class. It is a responsibility shared by all Christians. In accordance with Joel's prophecy, when God pours out His Spirit our sons and our daughters prophesy, our young men see visions and our old men dream dreams (Acts 2: 17). The outworking of this is seen in Acts 8: 4: 'Those who were scattered abroad went everywhere preaching the gospel.'

This already reminds us of the extensiveness of the church's mission. It is to embrace all the nations. It is against this background that we are to interpret the tongue-speaking of Pentecost. The church is to embrace, at last, people from every kindred, nation and tongue (Revelation 7: 9). If that objective is to be achieved the gospel must be preached in every tongue. That task was certainly not completed by the apostolic church. It remains as a target for each successive generation of Christians. Only when we reach it will the world be ready for the final form of the presence, the Parousia: 'The gospel must first be preached among all nations' (Mark. 13: 10).

Clearly, then, in the biblical account of Pentecost the privilege of the divine presence is related in the closest possible way to the evangelistic task of the church. As a Spirit of power and holiness God resides in the Christian community enabling and impelling it to proclaim in every tongue the wonderful works of God.

But this works two ways. If the church does not fulfil her

commission she forfeits the divine presence. The terms of Matthew 28: 19ff. are virtually contractual. Christ makes a conditional promise: 'If you go and teach, I am with you always. If you do not go and teach, I am not with you.' If the church ignores and violates the condition it has no right to expect the promise. It will end up precisely where the church at Laodicea ended up: 'Behold I stand at the door and knock' (Revelation 3 : 20). Christ was outside.

But there is something more important than even the connection between the presence and evangelism: the connection between the presence and holiness. It is precisely because God walks among us that we are to cleanse ourselves from all filthiness of the flesh and spirit, perfecting holiness in the fear of God (2 Corinthians 6: 16ff). In this passage the divine presence serves as an argument for holiness. But the connection is not merely by way of argument. It is more intimate than that. It is towards this goal that He leads us. And it is this fruit that He produces. To Him we owe any love, joy, peace, longsuffering, gentleness, meekness, goodness, faithfulness and self-control that we possess. When God is present in a life, such qualities are the inevitable result. Conversely, when God is absent, such a life is impossible.

Too often the presence of God is associated with gifts, power or comfort. These have their own importance. But they are not primary. What is primary is His presence as a Spirit of holiness and it is as such that we should seek and cherish Him. It is certainly as such that we have to live with Him.

CHAPTER SEVEN

GOD, RIGHTEOUSNESS AND RETRIBUTION

In virtually all the languages which have influenced the Christian tradition the basic idea of *right* and *righteous* appears to be *conformity to a given standard*. That standard might be a law or it might be a custom. In personal relationships, righteousness meant that one conformed to the rule which governed the relationship. One met its obligations. God's righteousness belongs to this same order of thought. He is faithful and predictable in all His relationships. There is therefore a very intimate connection between the idea of righteousness and the idea of the covenant, because the covenant, in one form or another, is always the norm of divine-human relationships. This connection is quite explicit in the Scriptures. We see it, for example, in Psalm 103: 17f: 'The mercy of the Lord is from everlasting to everlasting to them that fear him, and his righteousness unto children's children, to such as keep his covenant'. It appears again in Isaiah 42: 6: 'I the Lord have called thee in righteousness and will give thee for a covenant of the people'.

While it may be correct, then, to define righteousness as right conduct, the norm or standard of such conduct as far as God is concerned is always the covenant. The righteousness which characterises Him is always His faithfulness to His covenant; and the righteousness which He requires of us is that we should live according to His will as revealed in the covenant.

Retributive righteousness

There are two sides to this righteousness: retributive and remunerative.

Retributive righteousness means that God reacts to human conduct, both good and evil, with absolute propriety. He condones nothing; and He overlooks no mitigating or extenuating factor. At the most basic level, this retributive righteousness relates to God's covenant with Adam. Death reigns because in the first man all sinned. We repudiated the arrangement God made and He, utterly righteous, enacted the covenant curse: 'The day that thou eatest thereof, thou shalt surely die'

(Genesis 2: 17). But the sons of Adam are not mere innocent victims of his fatal disobedience. Each of us re-enacts his disobedience for himself. All men know God's will — some with the brilliant clarity of the New Testament revelation, some by the light of the Old Testament and some others by the light of nature. None can plead ignorance; and none lives up to the light he enjoys. Each of us knows more of God's will than he performs. The result is, again, that we come up against the covenant curse: 'Cursed is every one that continueth not in all things that are written in the book of the law to do them' (Galatians 3: 10).

Discretionary?

Some Reformed theologians have held that this retributive righteousness is discretionary. It was not an expression of God's essential nature but merely of His freely taken decision to punish sin. Samuel Rutherford, for example, wrote: 'God punishes sin by no necessity of nature. Nay, if He chose, He might leave it altogether unpunished' (Quoted in James Walker, *The Theology and Theologians of Scotland* 1560-1750, Edinburgh, 1982, p. 68).

John Owen disagreed and expressed his disagreement with uncharacteristic force and clarity: 'Of our own countrymen,' he writes, 'the only one I know who holds this view is Rutherford, a Scotch divine, who roundly and boldly asserts *'punitive justice to be a free act of the divine will'*. Nor is he content with the bare assertion, but he defends the fallacy against both Cameron and Voetius, those two thunderbolts of theological war; though in my opinion, neither with a force of argument nor felicity of issue equal to his opponents' (*Works*, Vol X, p. 507).

Owen was surely right. The reason that God visits sin with retribution is that He hates it and it is impossible to conceive of Him not hating it. He is of purer eye than to behold iniquity (Habakkuk 1: 13). All that He is reacts to it with anger and condemnation. One cannot go beyond this and ask, Why? It is His nature. The only variation the Scripture offers is to suggest that He punishes sin because this is absolutely right: 'Will not the Judge of all the earth do right?' (Genesis 18: 25). *Lawlessness* (John's definition of sin in 1 John 3:4) is radically offensive to God and He is no more capable of justifying wickedness than He is of condemning goodness. Indeed, to adopt either course would be to commit abomination (Proverbs 17: 15).

Modern Aversion

To many theologians today, this understanding of God is anathema. It was in fact what led John McLeod Campbell to dissent so strongly from the Calvinism of Owen and Edwards: 'The divine justice is conceived of by them as, by a necessity of the divine nature, awarding eternal misery to sin, and eternal blessedness to righteousness' (*The Nature of the Atonement*, Sixth Edition, London, 1915, p. 47). Campbell could not tolerate 'the conception of the fixed relation between sin and its due punishments'. His modern disciples — notably James B. Torrance — share his aversion, even to the extent of the same personal reference: 'The doctrine of a covenant of works implies that God is a contract-God, and denies that God is related to all men in love. John Owen and Jonathan Edwards took this to its logical conclusion that Justice is the essential attribute by which God is related to all as Judge, but the love of God is arbitrary!' (From an article *Strengths and Weaknesses of the Westminster Theology* in *The Westminster Confession in the Church Today*, Ed. Alasdair I.C. Heron, St. Andrew Press, Edinburgh, 1982, p. 48.) In a remarkably similar statement Torrance had written ten years earlier: 'McLeod Campbell saw — as in his discussion of the views of Owen and Jonathan Edwards in *The Nature of the Atonement* — that the doctrine of God was at stake. In the federal scheme, the justice of God is the essential attribute, and the love of God (or mercy of God) is an arbitrary attribute. All men are necessarily related to God as Judge in the framework of law, but only the elect are related to God by His love and mercy' *(The Scottish Journal of Theology*, Vol. 26, No. 3, p. 303).

Is it true, then, that the historic view of the righteousness of God (by no means confined to the Protestant theologians of the seventeenth century) contradicts His mercy? And is it true that while Owen and Edwards saw justice as essential, they regarded mercy as arbitrary and optional?

There are several things to be said.

First, Owen is emphatic that mercy belongs to the very being of God. 'We have laid it down as a fixed principle,' he writes, 'that mercy is essential to God. It is no less naturally inherent in God than justice.'

Secondly, Reformed theology, whether scholastic or not, has always recognised that the mercy of God extends to all men. This recognition was expressed particularly in the doctrine of Common Grace, which spoke unashamedly of 'a certain attitude of favour on God's part even towards the reprobate'. God exercised forebearance and long-suffering. He did not mark iniquity (Psalm 130: 3). He did not deal with men according to their sin. He sent His sun to shine and His rain to fall. He gave fruitful seasons. He provided a Saviour and pled with all men to come to Him.

Thirdly, an element of discretion or optionalness belongs to the idea of mercy by definition. (There is an excellent exposition of this theme in a sermon by W.G.T. Shedd entitled *The Exercise of Mercy Optional with God.* See *Sermons to the Natural Man, pp. 358-378.)* If mercy becomes something God is bound to dispense invariably and inevitably, it loses its distinctive quality entirely. Clemency is in its very nature sovereign.God has mercy on whom He will have mercy (Romans 9: 15). The beneficiary can only say, 'Even so, Father, for so it seemed good in thy sight' (Matthew 11: 26), while the observer exclaims, 'Oh, the depth, both of the wisdom and of the knowledge of God!' (Romans 11: 33). Far from being self-evident, the discovery of mercy evokes surprise and wonder. 'There is forgiveness!' exclaims the Psalmist (Psalms 130: 4), with all the joy of a man who has stumbled on something remarkable. Indeed, only a word from God can give us any assurance that there is such a thing as mercy, because the decision to exercise mercy — and, if so, to whom — and on what terms — lies entirely within the divine discretion. It is not, like His wrath, revealed from heaven (Romans 1: 18) or, like the certain doom of the reprobate, engraven indelibly upon their consciences (Romans 1: 32). It is a *mystery* — something eye has not seen, ear has not heard and the mind of man has not conceived (I Corinthians 2: 9). To forget this is to debase the currency of mercy: '*Dieu me pardonnera. C'est son metier.*' ('God will forgive me. It's His job.')

Fourthly, the antithesis between mercy and righteousness is a false one. The true opposite of mercy is not righteousness but cruelty and the true opposite of righteousness is not mercy but unrighteousness or injustice. In fact, righteousness is itself a function of love — a point made by someone as far removed from Reformed theology as Joseph Fletcher, the author of *Situation Ethics.* According to Fletcher, love and justice are the same: 'Justice is Christian love using its head, calculating its duties, obligations, opportunities, resources' (*Situation Ethics* S.C.M. Press, London, 1966, p. 95). A God who contemplated inhumanity with indifference or indulgence would not be loving. He would be amoral. And a universe presided over by One who would enact no sanctions against Belsen would not be lovely. It would be hell.

Fifthly, it is not true that according to historic orthodoxy God deals with all men on a basis of strict justice. In fact, God does not deal with anyone on such a basis. The aphorism that 'He is better to the worst of us than the best of us deserves' is fully warranted. Strict justice is departed from in the very first blessing of our earthly existence. 'Use every man after his desert,' said Hamlet, 'and who should 'scape whipping?' It is particularly misleading to suggest that God deals with His elect on a basis of strict justice. It is indeed true that we are accepted because of the righteousness of Christ. But the gift of Christ to be our Saviour is itself a matter of sheer grace, as is the faith which unites us to Him.

Sixthly, the punishment of sin is not itself unmerciful. If it were, then every conscientious judge would be unmerciful. The retort will be, of course, that God is a Father, not a Judge. That is less axiomatic than it looks. The idea of God as Judge pervades Scripture. Nor can we easily accept that our human justice — our jurisprudence — does not correspond to anything in God. The words of the philologist, Gottfried Quell, are worth pondering: 'That God posits law, and that He is bound to it as a just God, is a fundamental tenet in the Old Testament' (TDNT, Vol II, p. 176). 'Human justice has no validity except as it is a reflection or image of God's — which is probably why at one point in the Old Testament civil rulers are referred to as 'gods' (Psalm 82: 6)'.

This theme is developed by Professor T. F. Torrance in a stimulating booklet entitled *Juridicial Law and Physical Law* (Scottish Academic Press, Edinburgh, 1982). Professor Torrance argues that there are objective standards of civil and criminal law, just as there are objective standards in physics. Indeed, the laws of physics, the doctrines of theology and the principles of jurisprudence have a common source and belong to a unitary system. An act does not become right or wrong by decree of Parliament. On the contrary the duty of the legislature is not to *make* laws, but to *discover* them. Professor Torrance maintains that the great problem with our courts of law is that our judges lack 'a controlling sense of what is intrinsically true and right'. He adds, most significantly: 'The ground for this failure in legal vision into the essential justness of things, lies in the ontological uprooting of moral and juridical law from its objective ground in the ultimate Truth and Rightness of God Himself' (*op. cit.*, p. x). What Professor Torrance is saying here is that God is the archetypal Judge and that human jurisprudence is ultimately rooted in Him. Compare the words of Schrenk: 'The image of the judge is a tenable one because in legal life, however inadequately, imperishable divine norms are expressed' (TDNT, Vol. II, p. 205). If so, then our whole juridical process — including not only our verdicts and our sentences but also our decisions not to exercise clemency — correspond to a reality deep in God Himself. Indeed, if our human justice is not rooted in God, it has no validity and is in fact intolerable. Instead of this being the case, however, we find that the setting up of human judiciaries (to execute *His* wrath on evil-doers) is specifically ascribed to God Himself (Romans 13: 4). If such men may rightly condemn, without incurring the charge of being unmerciful, then so may God Himself, the source and norm of all our justice.

In the seventh place, Christ Himself clearly taught and exemplified the principle of retribution. We fully accept — indeed we would insist — that the Saviour must be the starting-point in all our reflection on the nature of God. He is the image of God's glory, a revelation precisely accurate in all its proportions, but adapted to our capacity. In Him, we see God loving the rich young ruler, weeping over the city and pleading with men to come to Him. But in Him we also see the money-lenders expelled from the Temple (John 2: 15); we see the fig tree cursed (Matthew 21: 19); we hear the direst woes pronounced on the Pharisees (Matthew 23: 13ff); we hear solemn words about a place of outer darkness (Matthew 8: 12). If it is not a contradiction of the mercy of Christ to anathematise and condemn, then it cannot be a contradiction of the mercy of God.

Finally, one has to say that if mercy and righteousness are mutually exclusive, the cross of Christ is inexplicable. When He enacted Calvary, had God ceased to be merciful? When He forsook His Son, did He no longer love Him? Why then did He deliver Him up? Why did He not spare Him? Why did He make Him sin? Why did He make Him a curse? Why did He not listen to the cry of dereliction and hasten to help? Of course He loved Him and of course He pitied Him and of course His heart was torn as He heard His Son plead that the cup might pass from Him! But there were other considerations. Christ had become — voluntarily — the sin-bearer; and God could not look on Him. God could not withhold the wages of sin. Calvary cannot be explained as an act of mercy. Nor dare we explain it as an act of cruelty and injustice — which, most assuredly, is what it looks like. It is a priestly act and as such an act of righteousness in which the divine holiness consumes the archetypal holocaust, doom-deserving as the vicar of His people. If, as Barth suggested, Christ is 'the judge judged in our place' (*Church Dogmatics*, T & T Clark, Edinburgh, 1956, p. 211 ff) then surely He was judged righteously? Otherwise, He was judged unrighteously. And what form did the unrighteousness take? Was it divine malice? That would be to turn the universe itself into a black-hole. The reputation of the God who delivered up His Son to the horrors of Calvary can only be redeemed if He acted on the ground of equity. It was right. It was consonant with those juridical norms which lie deep in the reality of God Himself. He reacts to the sin of the Last Adam as He did to the sin of the First — invoking the covenant anathema and expelling Him from His presence.

CHAPTER EIGHT

A JUST GOD AND A SAVIOUR

The retributive aspect of righteousness has obviously figured prominently in traditional theology. Indeed, it has often been the only aspect to receive attention. But it is only half the truth, if that. In Scripture the main emphasis falls on *remunerative* righteousness, that is, righteousness contemplated not as a reason for terror and alarm but as a ground of confidence and hope.

We find this view of the divine righteousness especially in the Psalms. Far from being intimidated by it, the psalmists appealed to it confidently: 'Hear me when I call, God of my righteousness' (Psalm 4: 1); 'Judge me, O Lord, according to thy righteousness' (Psalm 35: 24); 'In thy faithfulness answer, and in thy righteousness' (Psalm 143: 1). The same idea lies behind the prayer of Psalm 94: 2, 'Lift up thyself, thou *judge* of the earth'. If there is justice, the church has hope.

In the prophecies of Isaiah, God's righteousness is linked directly with the certainty of salvation. Indeed, the very existence of the nation was rooted in the righteousness of God: 'I am the Lord, I have called you in righteousness' (Isaiah 42: 6). This same covenant-faithfulness would lead to the redemption and restoration of Israel. This appears clearly in Isaiah 45: 8: 'Let the skies pour down righteousness: let the earth open, and let them bring forth salvation, and let righteousness spring up together'. We find the same thing in Isaiah 46: 13 and 51: 6. In the former God affirms, 'I bring near my righteousness: it shall not be far off, and my salvation shall not tarry'. In the latter He declares: 'My salvation shall be for ever, and my righteousness shall not be abolished'.

What is happening in all these passages is quite astonishing. Israel is building its confidence not on what *we* call grace but on what we call the righteousness of God. If God is straight, He will bless them; or, to change the perspective, their salvation is a matter of right or justice. It is rooted in final and absolute juridical norms.

But how can this be? The answer lies in the connection between righteousness and the covenant. God will be faithful to the relationship between Himself and Israel: and that relationship is defined by the covenant. They are Abraham's seed and therefore heirs to the promise, 'I will be God to thee and to thy seed after thee' (Genesis 17: 7).

The Old Testament

So far as the Old Testament people of God were concerned, this principle applied at four different levels.

It applied, first of all, when the nation collectively kept the covenant. Covenant- keeping would issue in covenant-blessing. This was made plain in Exodus 23: 22: 'If you listen carefully to what (Moses) says and do all that I say, I will be an enemy to your enemies and oppose those who oppose you'. Deuteronomy 28: 1 says the same thing: 'If you fully obey the Lord your God and carefully follow all his commands, the Lord your God will set you high above all the nations on earth'. And as a final example we may quote Deuteronomy 29: 9: 'Carefully follow the terms of this covenant, so that you may prosper in everything you do'. We must bear in mind that this kind of language does not mean that Israel's blessing depended on perfect obedience. The covenant between God and Israel cannot be identified exactly with the moral law. In fact, the covenant made on Sinai made explicit provision for dealing with sin. Israel could retain God's favour, even when it sinned, provided sin was dealt with in the way that the covenant stipulated. Offering the requisite sacrifices (including that of a broken and contrite heart) was part of the nation's covenant obedience.

Secondly, however, God's righteousness ensured that Israel was blessed even at times when the nation as a whole was unfaithful. At first glance this seems utterly paradoxical. But closer scrutiny shows that here too God was being entirely consistent. The apostasy of a single generation (or even more) cannot undo the covenant-keeping of the nation's fathers. This principle is clearly stated in connection with the Second Commandment: in contrast to His short-lived wrath (extending to only the third and fourth generation of those who hate Him) God's mercy extends to thousands of generations (Exodus 20: 5f.). This was the logic that lay behind the Exodus itself: 'God heard their groaning and he remembered his covenant with Abraham, with Isaac and with Jacob' (Exodus 2: 24). The psalmist had the same point of view: 'The mercy of the Lord is from everlasting to everlasting to them that fear him and his righteousness to children's children' (Psalm 103: 17). The most dramatic statement, however, is Paul's: they are beloved for the sake of their fathers (Romans 11: 28). Not even their rejection of the Messiah can undo the fact that Israel is special to God.

Thirdly, God's righteousness means covenant-blessing for Israel as represented by the remnant. This faithful remnant existed only as a result of God's gracious election (Romans 11: 5). They might walk in darkness and have no light, but they feared the Lord and heeded the word of His servants (Isaiah 50: 10). They were poor and afflicted, but they trusted in the name of the Lord. According to Zephaniah 3: 12ff, they would do no wrong, they spoke no lies and there would be no deceit found in their mouths. It was for them that the Great King described in Psalm 72 would act. God would give Him judgment and endow Him with righteousness (verse 1). So prepared, He would save the remnant (described according to their common earthly lot, as *the poor* and *the needy).* 'He shall deliver the needy when he crieth; the poor also, and him that hath no helper. He shall spare the poor and needy, and shall save the souls of the needy. He shall redeem their soul from deceit and violence: and precious shall their blood be in his sight' (verses 12-14). It is interesting to note that in verse 7 the beneficiaries described elsewhere as 'poor and needy' are referred to as 'the righteous': 'In His days shall the righteous flourish'. Even more intriguing is the close connection between remunerative and retributive righteousness indicated in verse 4: 'He shall judge the poor of the people, he shall save the children of the needy, and shall break in pieces the oppressor'. Salvation implies the destruction of His people's enemies. They shall lick the dust (Psalm 72: 9). This triumphalist theme runs right through Scripture. The Seed of the Woman shall crush the serpent's head (Genesis 3: 15). Christ triumphs over principalities and powers (Colossians. 2: 15), reigns until He makes His enemies His footstool (1 Corinthians 15: 25) and will eventually cast death and hell into the lake of fire (Revelation 20: 14).

Finally, individuals could turn to God's righteousness with the same confidence as the nation. This is clear, for example, in Psalm 35: 24: 'Judge me, O Lord, according to thy righteousness'. It appears again in Psalm 4:1, 'Hear me when I call, God of my righteousness' and particularly in Psalm 18: 20, 'The Lord rewarded me according to my righteousness; according to the cleanness of my hands hath he recompensed me'. The key to this confidence is the personal sense of covenant-keeping. This is at the furthest possible remove from legalism, however. It is a covenant faithfulness which loves the Lord, trusts Him and calls upon Him (Psalm 18: 1-3). It was also one which aspired to no high looks (Psalm 18: 27), frankly recognised the fact of sin and dealt with it in the way that God had prescribed.

The New Testament

The position in the New Testament is exactly the same. Paul defines the Good News in terms not of the grace but of the righteousness of God: 'I am not ashamed of the gospel of Christ, because in it the righteousness of God is revealed from faith to faith' (Romans 1: 16-17). This righteousness is the redemptive answer to the wrath revealed against all human ungodliness (Romans 1: 18). Similarly, Romans 5: 21 relates grace and righteousness in the closest possible way: 'Grace reigns through righteousness'. The process of redemption does not set aside God's integrity but (to express it in the words of Schrenk), 'God exercises grace which is not capricious but which is in accordance with His holy norms, with the covenant and with true right' (TDNT, Vol II, p. 205).

Nor is this understanding of righteousness confined to Paul. One of the clearest expressions of it is found in 1 John 1: 9: 'If we confess our sins, he is faithful (*pistos*) and righteous (*dikaios*) to forgive our sins and to cleanse us from all unrighteousness'. Here in a quite remarkable way the hope of forgiveness is rooted not in the mercy but in the righteousness of God. Remission is a matter of justice.

But how can this be? The answer lies in the doctrine of the atonement. What Christ did on Calvary has made it not only possible but mandatory for God to bless His people.

We can see this, for example, in Matthew 26: 28: 'This is my blood of the (new) covenant which is shed for many for the remission of sins'. Christ's suffering is covenant suffering, going back to the basic word spoken to the first Adam, 'The day thou eatest thereof, thou shalt surely die'. He becomes the great victim of the flaming sword that guards the way to the Tree of Life (Genesis 3: 24). He is made a curse, not arbitrarily or capriciously, but as the One who endures the covenant anathema. The covenant threat exhausts itself in Him: 'God condemned sin in the flesh of His own Son ' (Romans 8: 3). Therefore, in terms of the covenant itself, His people are immune. In Christ, in His obedience and suffering, they have met all the demands of the *dike* (God's standard), and their forgiveness is a matter of covenant right. It is a matter of the Father's covenant (contractual) obligation to Christ. Only derivatively is it *our* right.

These truths shine with even greater clarity in the great statement on reconciliation given in the closing verses of Second Corinthians Five. The whole initiative in reconciliation rests with God. It is an expression of His love: 'God was reconciling the world to himself'. But God's love is not itself reconciliation. Between love and reconciliation there lies the great transaction referred to in 2 Corinthians 5: 21: '(God) made him who knew no sin to be sin for us, so that we might become the righteousness of God in him'. There is a staggering amount of theology crammed into these few words. There is the sinlessness of Christ; there is the fact that whatever it was He suffered, God was the ultimate cause of it; and there is the fact that His suffering itself amounted to His being made sin. He bore it. He was identified with it. He was treated as it deserved to be treated — bruised for it (Isaiah 53: 10), accursed for it (Galatians 3: 13) and rejected for it (Mark 15: 34).

But how did Christ contract such sin? How did He become vulnerable to its retribution? What right did God have to bruise *Him*? Because He was *for* us. That made His condemnation — His expulsion to the Far Country — righteous. But then, beside the *for* there is another preposition, *in*. The *for* made Him guilty. The *in* makes us righteous: 'We are the righteousness of God *in* Him'. That is why God is reconciled to us — because we are righteous. That is why God justifies us — declares us righteous: because we *are* righteous. We have in Christ all the righteousness God can require. We are as righteous as Christ Himself. Indeed, we have God's own righteousness — we have kept the covenant as faithfully as God Himself.

We have seen, frequently, the close biblical connection between *righteousness* and *covenant*. Any exhaustive treatment would also have to show the connections with mercy, loving-kindness, truth and faithfulness. But we content ourselves with a brief allusion to a more vital connection still — that between righteousness and peace (*shalom*). It appears clearly in Psalm 85: 10, 'Righteousness and peace kiss each other'. In the day of the Great King, when righteousness flourishes, peace will abound (Psalm 72: 7). The connection is equally clear in the New Testament: 'Being justified (declared righteous) by faith, we have peace with God' (Romans 5: 1). The great symbol of this peace was the Dove who descended on our Lord at His baptism. The great seal of it is the indwelling of the Spirit in His fulness — the triune God in permanent residence in each one of His people. This *shalom* was the very heart of our Saviour's promise: 'Come, and I will give you rest'. We are delivered in Him from all our phobias; fear of our environment, fear of the future, fear of death, even from the neurotic fear of God. 'I will leave in the midst of you a poor and afflicted people. They shall feed and lie down and none shall make them afraid' (Zephaniah 3: 13).

CHAPTER NINE

THE HOLY OTHER

The Old Testament word for *holy* is QADOSH. Unfortunately, there is some uncertainty as to its derivation. According to some scholars, it comes from a Babylonian root meaning *to shine*. This suggests a connection between holiness and purity or brightness. Such an idea is in itself, of course, perfectly biblical; God is light (1 John 1: 5). The view taken by most scholars, however, is that QADOSH is derived from a Semitic root meaning *to cut off* or *to separate*. The holy is then, in the words of Eichrodt, 'that which is marked off, separated, withdrawn from ordinary use' (*Theology of the Old Testament,* Vol. I, p. 270). God is utterly different. He is separated from created existence in every possible form — separate from angels, separate from men and, above all, separate from sinners.

The way that the word *holy* is used in the Old Testament appears to confirm the view that its basic reference is to separation. It is applied, for example, to inanimate objects. There are holy garments (Exodus 28: 2), holy places (Exodus 29: 31), holy vessels (1Kings 8: 4) and holy instruments (Numbers 31: 6). This kind of holiness has nothing to do with moral and spiritual purity. It refers only to the fact that they are consecrated or set apart.

We can see this even more clearly if we note that throughout Scripture the holy means the opposite of the common or the profane. In Ezekiel 22: 26, for example, the Lord complains that 'the priests put no difference between the holy and the profane'. Similarly in Leviticus 20: 26, He says to Israel, 'Ye shall be holy unto me, for I the Lord am holy and have removed you from other people, that ye should be mine'.

There seems to be ample biblical justification, then, for defining holiness as the *otherness of God*; and even for Rudolf Otto's description of the Creator as 'the wholly other'. (*The Idea Of The Holy*, Penguin Books, London, 1959, p. 39ff). God is 'quite beyond the sphere of the usual, the intelligible and the familiar'. He falls outside the range of familiar, manageable objects. He is uncanny.

The otherness of God

In what does this otherness consist?

First, in the incomprehensibility of God. Even when He reveals Himself, He remains a mystery. Indeed, He reveals Himself as a mystery, so that a soul confronted with the words which God has spoken about Himself is compelled to cry out, 'Oh! the depth of the riches both of the wisdom and of the knowledge of God! How unsearchable are his judgments and his ways past finding out!' (Romans 11: 33). He reveals His own incomprehensibility, pointing us in His Word to facets of His being which to us are utterly unfathomable. It is not only *how big He is* but *the way that He is* which defies our categories and transcends our understanding. We cannot grasp self-existence or triuneness or eternalness. There is a terrifying unfamiliarity in the things that God says about Himself.

The second element in God's otherness is His supremacy. He is *the high* and holy one — God most High — possessing a final and unchallengeable authority. He is not *irresponsible* but He is non-responsible — answerable to no one. In the words of the Westminster Confession (II: II): 'God hath most sovereign dominion over all things, to do by them, for them or upon them whatsoever Himself pleaseth'. It is surely because of this absolute finality of His will that God is the one 'from whose face the earth and the heaven fled away' (Revelation 20: 11). It is for this same reason that God's command is of categorical authority. In Him, we confront ultimate — and therefore absolutely different — obligation. We cannot evade it or appeal against it. His *ought* binds us unconditionally.

Thirdly, God is other in His power. We ourselves are powers and we are conscious of other men as powers. But in God we meet a different kind of power. It is different in its being eternal (Romans 1: 20). It is different too in its sheer magnitude. Out of nothing, it creates a universe of immeasurable vastness and complexity. By its very word, it upholds all things (Hebrews 1: 3). Above all, God's power is terrifyingly different in its destructive capability. With the same ease as it creates it can destroy, pulling the universe apart and causing the elements to melt with fervent heat (2 Peter 3: 12). Man is often conscious that this power stands over him threateningly. 'He breaketh me with a tempest,' exclaims Job in his anguish, 'and will not suffer me to take my breath. If we speak of strength, lo! he is strong' (Job 9: 17ff). Even when the revelation is gracious, the impression of sheer, threatening might is overwhelming, forcing Isaiah, for example, to cry, 'Woe is me! for I am undone!' (Isaiah 6: 5).

Another factor in God's otherness is His purity. The biblical allusions to this are innumerable. In God there is no darkness at all (1 John 1: 5). He is of purer eyes than to behold evil (Habakkuk 1: 13) and the very stars are not 'pure in His sight' (Job 25: 5). This purity is of such brilliance that even the sinless seraphim cover their faces with their wings (Isaiah 6: 2). For man, the sinner, the difference is even more intense — and painful. We walk in darkness and *are* darkness and even *love* the darkness. It is no joy, then, when our iniquities are set before God and the sins of our secrecy placed in the unbearable light of His countenance (Psalm 90: 8).

Yet again, God's otherness means that He is unapproachable. Our sense of this does not arise only from our being sinners. It is already involved in our being creatures. Isaiah's seraphim cannot look at God (Isaiah 6: 2).The Fall only widens and deepens an existing gulf. The way to the tree of life is guarded against man by the flaming sword of the divine anathema (Genesis 3: 24). Every penitent and every worshipper must remember that. The way back to God was closed even against the last Adam (Man). To return to the Father He had to encounter the flaming sword and become a curse instead of us (Galatians 3: 13). It is this fact of the unapproachableness of God that underlies the whole elaborate ritual of the Mosaic administration. God can be approached; but only through the *cultus*. One can come only through a priest, only at an appointed place and only at an appointed time. Above all, one can approach only through blood. Access, in other words, is jealously guarded by an elaborate protocol and the terrible consequences of defying it appear in the story of Korah and his associates, destroyed because they tried to approach Jehovah in an unauthorised way (Numbers 16: 1-35).

This emphasis on the unapproachableness of the Lord is modified in the New Testament, but it by no means disappears. The right to come to God cannot be taken for granted. It belongs only to those who are justified by faith (Romans 5: 2) and is possible at all only because we have a great High Priest (Hebrews 4: 14). Indeed, the supreme achievement of Christ is that He is the Way — the only way — to God; and He is that only through His broken humanity — the rent veil of His own flesh (Hebrews 10: 20).

One other detail may be added. God is other in His grace. Grace is often contrasted with holiness, but the contrast is unwarranted and is only possible because we commit the elementary theological blunder of taking grace for granted. That is totally improper. It is precisely in His grace that the Old Testament sees the incomparableness of Jehovah. In this quality, He is totally different from every pagan deity — and from every conclusion of natural theology: 'Who is a God like thee, who pardons iniquity and passes by the transgression of the remnant of his heritage?' (Micah 7: 18).

But if, on the one hand, God is distinguished from the other gods by the very fact of His grace, then He is distinguished from man by the sheer scale of His grace. What man forgives is as nothing compared to what God forgives; and no gift of ours can possibly compare with God's extravagance in not sparing His own Son but delivering Him up for us all (Romans 8:32). Nor can we hope to match the prodigality that 'hyper-exalts' us — lifting us out of the depths of depravity and degradation and making us possessors of the very glory which Christ had with the Father before the world was (John 17: 5). There is the heart of the otherness of God, confounding the expectations of the human conscience not only by exercising forbearance but by lavishing on us the glory of His grace — even filling us with all the fulness of God (Ephesians 3: 19). No wonder that Isaiah (followed by Paul) exclaims, 'Eye hath not seen nor ear heard, neither have entered into the heart of man, the things that God hath prepared for those that love him' (Isaiah 64: 4).

Fear and Fascination

What response should this holiness of God evoke?

First, fear. Otto's phrase, *mysterium tremendum* is useful here (*op. cit.* p. 26ff). God is tremendous in the strictest sense that He makes us tremble. His presence sends a tremor through us. He is awesome, threatening, overwhelming. Isaiah, confronted with the reality of God, feels dreadfully vulnerable: 'Woe is me! I am destroyed!' (Isaiah 6: 5). Jacob's experience at Bethel was exactly the same. Jehovah was in the place, 'and he was afraid, and said, How full of dread is this place' (Genesis 28: 17). For the same reason God is called 'the Fear of Isaac' (Genesis 31: 42) and religion itself designated 'the fear of the Lord' (Proverbs 1: 7; 19: 23). There is something here elemental, even primitive, and yet indispensable to Christian piety, even (perhaps especially) when united with the fullest possible assurance of the divine love for ourselves. Our Father is *in heaven*: and that heavenliness fills us with what Otto called 'creature-feeling'. It makes us feel like nonentities. It makes us feel totally incompetent. It is unmanageable, eerie and uncanny so that involuntarily the goose pimples rise on our skin and our instinct (unless modified either by grace or by presumption) is to turn and flee.

But then, paradoxically, man is also fascinated (we are still using the terminology of Otto, who spoke of God as not only *tremendum* but as *fascinans*). The very vision which intimidates and repels also draws and attracts: 'I will turn aside and see this great sight' (Exodus 3: 3). There is a fascination in the very unfamiliarity of God and a compelling loveliness in His matchless purity. This is why man's attitude to Him has been so ambivalent. On the one hand, there has been undoubted revulsion and enmity. On the other, there has been the God-shaped void in the heart of man, impelling to recognition and religion. Even in his flight, man has looked back, obsessed with the object of his fear. But what is morbid in the unbeliever is the very vitality of the believer. Faith sees the beauty of His holiness and in seeing Him is blessed. Vision (of God) is beatific. The theme is common in the Scriptures. The one thing the writer of Psalm 27 longs for is to dwell continually in the house of Jehovah so that he can gaze and gaze and gaze upon His beauty (verse 4). The promise to the pure in heart is that they shall see God (Matthew 5: 8). Similarly, Paul longs for the day when he will see Christ not through a glass, darkly (literally, as an enigma) but face to face (1 Corinthians 13: 12). (The paradox of this must not be lost on us. At one level, we cannot see His face and live. At another, we live by seeing His face.) John has the same outlook, longing to see Him as He is (1 John 3: 2). His great comfort in the midst of all the plagues and famines and persecutions is that he can see the Lamb in the midst of the throne (Revelation 5: 6). The light is such as we can walk with (1 John 1: 7) and such as illuminates, most benignly, the heavenly city. The consuming fire is the light of Paradise (Revelation 21: 23).

The Holy One in the midst of us

Any reflection on the practical implications of the holiness of God must begin by remembering that He is not only the Holy One: He is the Holy One '*in the midst of you*' (Isaiah 12: 6). God's separateness does not mean that He cannot be present with us. He is with us, around us, even *in* us. Our bodies are His temple, our congregations His dwelling-place. But we can never forget that He is present as 'the Holy One'. He does not allow His involvement to compromise or contaminate Him. Nor have we any right to interpret His nearness as a sign that He has relaxed His standards and is prepared to condone sin. The One who is with us is dreadful. This is why it is fair to say that right through the Old Testament it was a terrible strain to be an Israelite. The Divine Visitor was not easy to live with and the protocol required by His presence was exceedingly burdensome. At almost every point life was hedged in with what could easily be regarded as irksome restrictions. Flagrant breaches of the protocol — such as those of Achan and Korah — brought terrible retribution. But quite apart from these, the special relationship with God involved grave risks: 'You only have I known of all the families of the earth: therefore I will punish you for all your iniquities' (Amos 3: 2).

It would be unfair to claim that the New Testament teaching is precisely the same. We are now living in 'the fulness of the times' (Galatians 4: 4). It is very doubtful whether this has any reference to the preparation for the gospel (the so-called *praeparatio evangelica*). True as it was that at the time of the Advent the world was ready for Christ (through the dispersion of the Jews, the prevalence of the Roman peace and the widespread use of Greek as a common language), that is not the point. The fulness of the times is the moment destined by God for the church to emerge out of its minority into adulthood. In the New Testament we are no longer treated like children. We have come of age, with all the privileges and responsibilities which that brings. We have greater intimacy with God. We have a new freedom. Above all, we are no longer under the burden of Mosaic restrictions. God has cast away these weak and beggarly elements and forbidden us to be entangled again with the yoke of bondage (Galatians 5: 1).

Yet, however momentous this transition from the old dispensation to the new, it would be perilous to assume that our relations with God can now be relaxed and easy. The New Testament is full of evidence to the contrary. The tension between presence and holiness is already evident in the incarnation itself. Christ is both Emmanuel 'God with us' and 'the holy one' (Matthew 1: 23; Luke 1: 35). The account of the Spirit's coming at Pentecost continues this stress on the holiness of the presence. The cloven tongues 'as if of fire' (Acts 2: 3) are reminiscent of the burning bush, the pillar of fire and the fire that consumed the two hundred and fifty followers of Korah (Numbers 16: 35). All of these are symbols of the divine purity and majesty, reacting destructively to sin in the church. The same principle is illustrated even more dramatically in the story of Ananias and Sapphira (Acts 5: 1-11). They lied to the God who was in and with the church and their fate underlines the fact that in the New Testament, as in the Old, living with God involves great strain and serious risk. The presence of God involves for us, as for Israel, the possibility of chastisement: 'As many as I love I rebuke and chasten' (Revelation 3: 19). It is for this reason that sometimes the presence (*parousia*) of God is not a promise but a most solemn threat. Amos, for example, protests against the facile, ill-considered longing for divine intervention by crying, 'The day of the Lord is darkness and not light!' (Amos 5: 20). Even more paradoxically, the risen Christ sends to the backslidden church of Ephesus the message, 'Repent or I come quickly' (Revelation 2: 5). For all the transition from the Old Testament to the New, then, fear remains an integral element in our relations with God: 'If you call on the Father, who without partiality judges according to every man's work, pass the time of your sojourn here in fear' (1 Peter 1: 17). Not even the greatest confidence in saying, 'Abba, Father!' can eliminate the sense of holy dread inalienable from man's approach to God. Even Christ pauses on the threshold and says '*Holy* Father' (John 17: 11). Even as *our* God, He is a consuming fire (Hebrews 12: 29).

Practical implications

This fact of the presence of the Holy One among us is the basis of three practical principles.

First, 'Be ye holy, for I am holy'. At one level, our holiness is the condition of His presence. Our unholiness repels Him. But the reasoning is probably deeper than that. To be unholy is to run the risk of causing His wrath to burn — not now from the comparative remoteness of Mt Sinai but from within ourselves. His anger will burn in His temple — 'which temple ye are' (1 Corinthians 3: 16f). But why will His anger burn so fiercely against His own people — more fiercely against them than against 'the rest'? Because their unholiness compromises Him. He is their God. They bear His name. They must therefore hallow it; and when they do not, He is jealous for the sake of His name.

Secondly, the vision of God's holiness is the basis of Christian service. We usually find the basis of our evangelism in the perception of human need and this is not to be dismissed as altogether irrelevant. But it is not the main emphasis of Scripture. Time and again the Bible indicates that the true constraint to prophetic testimony is an overwhelming and abiding vision of the holiness of God. It was so in the case of Isaiah — he 'goes' because he has seen the Lord high and lifted up (Isaiah 6: 1). Similarly, compliance with 'the great commission' springs from the vision of the Lord as the One who has all the authority in heaven and in earth (Matthew 28: 18). In the same way, Paul preached Christ among the Gentiles because it had 'pleased God to reveal His Son in me' (Galatians 1: 16) — a revelation of such overwhelming force that it had laid him prostrate and helpless on the Damascus Road.

Finally, the holiness of God must regulate and inform our worship. We are approaching the august and majestic One. Our approach cannot, therefore, be flippant or trivial. It must be tremulous and respectful, even in its moments of greatest boldness. We must come with pure hearts and sprinkled consciences (Hebrews 10: 22). Above all we must realise that we approach only by invitation, and that the important thing is not that we come in a way that we find enjoyable or entertaining but that we come in the spirit, attitude and posture that He commands. Our Father, indeed: but our *heavenly* Father.

CHAPTER TEN

DIVINE ANGER

The idea of the divine wrath has all but disappeared from preaching today. To some extent this is a matter of mood and sentiment. As James Packer points out, 'The subject of divine wrath has become taboo in modern society and Christians by and large have accepted the taboo and conditioned themselves never to raise the matter' (*Knowing God*, Hodder and Stoughton, London, 1973, p. 164). But the mood has found at least some justification in theological argument. C.H. Dodd, in particular, used his impressive scholarship to mount a sustained attack on the traditional Christian understanding. Divine anger, he maintained, was a pagan idea, inapplicable to the Christian God. He even suggested that we should speak of the *wrath of God* rather than the *anger of God* because the archaic phrase suited a thoroughly archaic idea (*The Epistle of Paul to the Romans,* Fontana Books, London, 1959, p. 47). In fact, to speak of it as merely archaic was an understatement. The idea was positively primitive: 'It is only to a God not yet fully conceived in terms of moral personality that the primitive numinous terror can be directed. The idea of an angry God is a first attempt to rationalise the shuddering awe which men feel before the incalculable possibilities of appalling disaster inherent in life, but it is an attempt which breaks down as the rational element in religion advances. In the long run we cannot think with full consistency of God in terms of the highest ideals of personality and yet attribute to Him the irrational passion of anger' (*op. cit.*, p. 50).

If Dodd were correct we should have to throw away large sections of the Bible and completely rewrite Christianity. But before dismissing him altogether we should note the truth reflected in his arguments. The God of Israel, the God and Father of our Lord Jesus Christ, *is* different from pagan deities: and among other things He is different in His wrath. For example, the Bible makes very clear that God is angry only reluctantly. He delights in mercy and loves forgiving. By contrast, judgment is a 'strange work'. He will resort to it if need be, but it is alien to His instincts. He is slow to wrath (Psalm 103: 8) and unwilling to afflict (Lamentations 3: 33). Even as He contemplates those who are steeped in guilt He hesitates to execute judgment: 'How shall I give thee up, Ephraim? How shall I deliver thee, Israel? My heart is turned within me. I will not execute the fierceness of mine anger, I will not return to destroy Ephraim' (Hosea 11: 8f.). The salvation of His people fills the Lord with joy (Jude 24). But the destruction of the wicked gives Him no pleasure (Ezekiel 18: 23, 32).

It is not simply a question of the asymmetry between wrath and grace, however. The anger of the living God differs in its very nature from that of the pagan deities. They were irascible and malicious, petty and egotistical. Their anger was capricious, arbitrary and unpredictable. One never knew when they might 'see red'. They were beings of ungovernable passion, their anger no different from that of ill-tempered human beings. It was a matter of whim and fury. In the Scriptures the wrath of God is deliberately contrasted with such behaviour. The Writer to the Hebrews, for example, reminds us that human fathers chastise their children 'according to their own pleasure' (12: 10). Their comfort or their ego is threatened, they get into a foul mood, they blow a fuse and lash out. God never behaves like that. If He corrects His children, it is for their own good . If He judges, it is in equity. He is not going to destroy cities, uproot civilisations and send men to Hell because of a mood. He will do it only if it is right. His anger, like all His dealings with men, is covenantal. He has made His stipulations unmistakably plain and left men and women in no doubt as to the consequences of defiance. His wrath will operate only within that framework: only against disobedience, only after the rejection of forgiveness and only after He has taken into account everything we have to say in mitigation.

But none of this can detract from the fact that the wrath of God is a reality in both the Old Testament and the New. There can be no peaceful co-existence between God and sin. Where He sees lawlessness, godlessness and inhumanity, He cannot but react with the profoundest aversion. It is His very nature to vindicate sin's victims and destroy its perpetrators. If it were not (if He reacted equally to virtue and vice) He would not be a moral being at all and the universe would have no moral foundation. Indeed, if we mean by universe 'structured, ordered, reality', we would have no universe at all. Paradoxically, a God without anger would be the end of all hope because He could preside only over a world without meaning.

The biblical evidence against Dodd is, at least on the face of things, overwhelming. As Leon Morris points out, the Old

Testament uses 20 different words to describe the divine wrath and the concept itself occurs over 580 times (*The Apostolic Preaching of the Cross*, Tyndale Press, London, 1960, p. 131). The New Testament evidence is equally impressive. The divine anger is prominent in all strands of the tradition, including the Synoptic Gospels.

Sub-Christian

But Dodd has an answer to this: in fact, two answers.

One is to dismiss as sub-Christian all passages which speak of the anger of God. This is obviously the easiest way of dealing with the Old Testament material: it was pre-rational and would disappear as the rational element in religion advanced. But Dodd applied the same procedure to sections of the New Testament, especially to the *Revelation of John*, where the idea of the divine anger is particularly prominent and where we meet the concept of 'the Wrath of the Lamb' (Revelation 6: 16). It would be difficult to think of a bolder way of giving a Christian endorsement to the concept of divine wrath. But Dodd will have none of it. To him, *The Revelation* is a sub-Christian book, its whole tone and temper the result of a relapse into pre-Christian eschatology: 'With all the magnificence of its imagery and the splendour of its visions of the majesty of God and the world to come, we are bound to judge that in its conception of the character of God and His attitude to man the book falls below the level, not only of the teaching of Jesus, but of the best parts of the Old Testament. The God of the Apocalypse can hardly be recognised as the Father of our Lord Jesus Christ, nor has the fierce Messiah, whose warriors ride in blood up to their horses' bridles, many traits that could recall Him of whom the primitive *kerygma* proclaimed that He went about doing good' (*The Apostolic Preaching and its Developments*, Hodder & Stoughton, London, 1967, p. 40f).

But what right do we as Christians have to stand in judgment over our Canon and pronounce some parts 'better', and whole books sub-Christian? If John's understanding of the character of God is wrong, what is left? If we are not prepared to yield to any canon but our own pre-conceived notions of what is Christian, what is left? And what are we to do with those magnificent portions of the Apocalypse which, far from falling below the level of other parts of the Bible, tower majestically over them? Are we to forfeit the great vision of the Lamb in the midst of the Throne (Revelation 5: 6), which so splendidly irradiates the sovereignty of God with the light of the incarnation? Are we to dispense with the notion of the Lamb shepherding the church (Revelation 7: 17) and do away with the picture of the City which has no need of the Sun 'because the glory of God lightens it and the Lamb is the Light thereof' (Revelation 21: 23)? To be a Christian means, if it means anything, accepting the word of the apostles as the Word of God. That being so, there is no place (at least, not within discipleship) for subjecting their teaching to the judgment of our prejudices as to what is Christian. On the contrary, it is our idea of what is Christian that must be judged by their teaching.

Is the Wrath personal?

Dodd's second response is to argue that in the fully-developed teaching of Scripture the Wrath was not something personal but an abstract law of cause and effect: "'The Wrath' meant, not a certain feeling or attitude of God towards us, but some process or effect in the realm of objective facts' (*The Epistle of Paul to the Romans*, p. 48). He puts it more chillingly in another volume: "'The Wrath of God', therefore, as seen in actual operation, consists in leaving sinful human nature to 'stew in its own juice'" (*The Meaning of Paul for Today*, Collins, London, 1958, p.67). It was not *God's* wrath at all but only a cosmic law to the effect that sin is always followed by disaster.

For all Dodd's eminence it is difficult to take this seriously. The arguments against it are formidable.

First: abstract, impersonal law of the kind envisaged here is a complete fiction. If the laws of physics have no independent status but are only 'the customs of God', how much more the laws of retribution! If sin is followed by disaster, by whom is that sequence established, if not by God? If sinful men are left to 'stew in their own juice', who leaves them? We do not soften the idea one whit by suggesting that God so leaves them *impersonally*. In a world where even the fall of a sparrow is part of His providence it is difficult to see how the punishment of sin can be outwith His jurisdiction. Even if He did do no more than stand idly by while the law of retribution took effect in the lives of His creatures, that would imply an attitude (and a very personal attitude) on His part. But of course He does not stand idly by: 'God,' wrote Karl Barth, 'is the Lord in all His rule, even in that of His wrath and the destruction and perdition which it brings. He Himself determines the course and direction and meaning of it: not some necessity immanent to its occurrence. How God will fulfil the sentence to which man has fallen inescapably victim is a matter for Him to decide' (*Church Dogmatics*, IV. I, p.221).

Secondly: the biblical writers portray the anger of God in the most intensely personal terms. Dodd makes much of the fact that Paul sometimes speaks of *The Wrath* 'in a curiously impersonal way' (Romans 2: 5, Romans 9: 22, Ephesians 2: 3). He makes even more of the fact that Paul never uses the verb *to be angry* with God as subject. But such arguments are more clever than convincing. In Romans 1: 18-32, for example, the anger is clearly personal. It is the wrath *of God* and it leads to the action of which He is very much the subject: God gave them over to impurity (verse 24), God gave them over to shameful lusts (verse 26), God gave them over to a reprobate mind (verse 28). This kind of thinking is carried over into chapter 2. On the day of God's wrath, *He* will give to each person according to what he has done and the 'trouble and distress' allocated to the wicked will be just as much *His* as the glory, honour and immortality allocated to the righteous (Romans 2: 9).

When we look at the rest of Scripture we see a similar picture. All the writers speak of the wrath in vividly personal terms. Amos asks boldly, 'Shall evil befall the city and the Lord hath not done it?' (Amos 3: 6). What could be more personal than the words of Ezekiel 7: 8f: 'Now I will shortly pour out my fury upon thee and accomplish mine anger against thee. And mine eye shall not spare, neither will I have pity. And ye shall know that I, the Lord, do smite'. Even the prophets who spoke most movingly and most originally of the divine love also spoke unashamedly of the wrath. Isaiah, for example, portrays God as declaring, 'I will tread down the people in mine anger and make them drunk in my fury, and I will bring down their strength to the earth' (Isaiah 63: 6). And in Hosea, the great preacher of the loving-kindness of the Lord, God protests: 'I will be unto Ephraim as a lion, and as a young lion to the house of Judah; I, even I, will tear and go away; I will take away, and none shall rescue him' (Hosea 5: 14).

The anger of Jesus

Dodd, as we have seen, cited the example of Jesus as an argument against the teaching of the Book of Revelation. But this is totally unwarranted. Apart altogether from His teaching,

Jesus Himself was, on occasion, thoroughly angry. For example, when He healed the man with the withered hand (in the synagogue, and on the Sabbath day) we are told that He looked around at the hostile, hypocritical spectators in anger (Mark 3: 5). Sometimes, even when there is no explicit allusion to anger, the Lord's actions clearly reflect this passion. How else can we understand the purging of the Temple? 'Get these out of here! How dare you turn my Father's house into a market!' (John 2: 16). This is particularly important in view of the fact that, as H.R. Mackintosh pointed out, 'All that Jesus did and said was revelation. His tears are God's mercy, His wrath God's anger' (*The Christian Experience of Forgiveness*, Nisbet, London, 1961, p. 88). The divine anger is as personal as Jesus Himself. If He was capable of it then there can be nothing in it unworthy of the most highly developed moral personality.

There is at least one further point worth pondering: it is only because the Wrath is personal that mercy and forgiveness are possible. If the divine wrath were an impersonal law of cause and effect, operating inexorably within history and ensuring invariably that all sin was followed by commensurate disaster, then indeed we would have reason to exclaim, 'Who shall stand!' In the very nature of the case, such a law could show no mercy. Every civilisation would then be given over to a reprobate mind and every sinner tormented by cosmic retribution. Suppose that at last God could stand the spectacle of His anguished creation no longer and rose to intervene, what could He do? He could not propitiate or appease such a law. He could only abolish it: and even that could be achieved only by changing the structure of reality itself. The remission of sins would be as impossible as a square circle because the very shape of the universe would demand that men be left to 'stew in their own juice'.

In the traditional Christian teaching, on the other hand, anger is an attribute of the living, personal God, who is able to form personal relationships and make personal responses. It is this which makes propitiation, reconciliation and forgiveness possible: 'Though *thou* wast angry with me, *thine* anger is turned away and *thou* comfortedst me' (Isaiah 12: 1).

We certainly need to be careful how we define God's wrath, purging it of all that is pagan and of all that reflects our own sinful humanity. But we have no right to eliminate it from our message. It is an integral part of the Bible's portrait of the living God.

Against Whom?

But against whom does this wrath operate? We think, instinctively, against the lost in Hell. But this is far from the whole truth.

For example, within history God expresses His anger against nations and even against whole civilisations. This is a recurring theme in the Old Testament, particularly in connection with such incidents as the Deluge (Genesis 6: 5ff.), the destruction of Sodom and Gomorrah (Genesis 19: 24) and the long series of judgments on Israel's neighbours announced in Amos 1: 2 - 2: 3. But it is taught with particular clarity in Romans. 1: 18ff. : 'The wrath of God is revealed from heaven against all ungodliness and unrighteousness of men'. The peculiar thing here is that the anger is expressed not in physical and economic calamities but in moral collapse. Paul is not teaching that one day God will punish Roman civilisation for its vice and decadence. On the contrary, the vice and decadence are themselves God's punishment. Provoked by their idolatry, He gave them over to shameful lusts and to depraved minds. Their punishment *was* their greed, envy, strife, deceit, violence and faithlessness.

Those of us who are not apostles cannot speak with Paul's confidence of God's judgment within history. But it is safe to assume that every human system which forgets its own dependence and accountability, will, sooner rather than later, be shattered by the divine anger. It seems safe, too, to see in the current world-wide prevalence of violence and vice exactly the same phenomenon as Paul describes in Romans One. They are not to be seen as things which will one day render us liable to the wrath. They are clear proof that the wrath is already being poured out.

Against His Own Children

But God's anger is by no means reserved exclusively for the godless. Scripture makes very plain that it is frequently directed against His own children. In fact in the Old Testament the vast majority of the references are to God's wrath either against Israel or against individual members of the covenant community. The principle which underlay this was expressed fearlessly by Amos: 'You only have I known of all the families of the earth: therefore I will punish you for all your iniquities' (Amos 3: 2). What is meant in practice may be gathered from the anguished words of Daniel: 'He hath fulfilled his words, which he spoke against us, and against our judges that judged us, by bringing upon us a great evil; for under the whole heaven has not been done as has been done upon Jerusalem' (Daniel 9: 12).

The same point is made frequently in the New Testament. In 1 Peter 1: 17, for example, it is precisely those who call on God as Father whom Peter exhorts to live in reverent fear. Why? Because even in the running of His own family God is an impartial judge. The idea becomes explicit in Revelation 3: 19, 'As many as I love I reprove and chasten'. It is spelt out fully in Hebrews 12: 5ff: 'For whom the Lord loves, he chastens, and scourges every son whom he receives'. Those who are not sons escape correction: that itself is proof that they are illegitimate (Hebrews 12: 8).

As we have already seen there is nothing irrational or capricious in God's chastening: 'He disciplines us for our good, that we may be partakers of his holiness'. Yet the severity of God's anger, even with His children, should not be underestimated. It is precisely as *our* God that He is a consuming fire (Hebrews 12: 29); and precisely for *us* that it is a terrible thing to fall into the hands of the living God (Hebrews 10: 31). His discipline is not joyous, but grievous (Hebrews 12: 11), and will frequently test us to the very limit of our resources. This will be especially true when we cannot see its purpose and when its only apparent effect is to leave us embittered and exhausted. Sometimes, in the midst of suffering, believers may have Job's confidence that they will come forth as gold (Job 23: 10). More often it is only afterwards that they can see that their anguish produced a harvest of righteousness (Hebrews 12: 11). In the meantime they must try to remember that God's great concern is not our happiness but our holiness and that He will not shrink from whatever is necessary to secure it.

Children of wrath?

In Ephesians. 2: 3, Paul speaks of believers as having been, by nature, *children of wrath* and the phrase has sometimes caused difficulty for those who believe in God's eternal election of His people. How could the children of God ever be children of wrath?

It is, of course, true (and monumentally important) that the people of God were known and loved and chosen before the foundation of the world. God's love for His own is eternal: He never existed without loving them. What Paul is speaking of, however, is what they were *by nature*. By nature, wrath is what they deserved. Indeed, it is what they still, by nature, deserve and will always deserve until God Himself makes them faultless (Jude 24). Furthermore, we must not lose sight of the historical aspects of salvation. The church was loved and chosen eternally, but it was not redeemed eternally. It was redeemed in the visible, audible, tangible, bloody transaction on Calvary, under Pontius Pilate. Similarly, justification and adoption are historical, not eternal, acts. We are justified by faith in Christ and until we actually exercise such faith we are condemned sinners, under the wrath of God. The same is true of adoption. It is linked indissolubly to faith: 'As many as received him, to them gave he authority to become children of God' (John 1: 12). Until we receive Him, we are *not* children of God. We are enemies and aliens.

The solemn truth is that God has elect and beloved ones who do not yet belong to the fold (John 10:16). Only when His eternal purpose is fulfilled in history through the new birth and conversion do the elect actually receive forgiveness and become members of the family of God.

The wrath to come

However important it is to remember that God's wrath expresses itself within history (against believers as well as against unbelievers) there can be no doubt that it is at the end of history that it finds its most awesome expression. 'The wrath to come' (Matthew 3: 7, 1 Thessalonians 1: 10) will effect the destruction and perdition of the whole community of 'ungodly men' (2 Peter 3: 7). But certain groups are identified specifically. John the Baptist, for example, singles out 'the brood of vipers': those Jews who thought that mere physical descent from Abraham would secure their immunity from judgment, regardless of the inhumanity and hypocrisy of their life-style. 'Who', he asks, 'warned you to flee from the wrath to come?' (Matthew 3: 7). Paul singles out those who do not obey the gospel (2 Thessalonians 1; 8), probably a reference to apostate Christians. Jesus for His part made very plain that the divine anger will fall with special severity on those who had unusual spiritual privileges and yet persisted in unbelief: 'And that servant who knew his Lord's will, and prepared not himself, neither did according to his will, shall be beaten with many stripes' (Luke 12: 47). The point is made more dramatically in Matthew 11: 20ff., especially in verses 22 and 24: on the day of judgment it will be more tolerable for Tyre and Sidon,

Sodom and Gomorrah, than for those who witnessed Christ's mighty acts and yet rejected Him.

The divine anger clearly presupposes that all men know something of the will of God. Some know more of it than others. But all know more than they perform.

The New Testament references to the wrath to come give remarkable prominence to Christ. For example, in 2 Thessalonians 1: 7 it is the Lord Jesus who is to be revealed from heaven in flaming fire, punishing those who defy the gospel. We have already seen the same idea in the Book of Revelation, where men call to the mountains and to the rocks, 'Fall on us and hide us from the wrath of the Lamb!' (6: 16). But the idea goes right back to the teaching of the Lord Himself. In Matthew 7: 23, it is He who says to the evil-doers, 'Depart from me! I never knew you!' And repeatedly throughout this gospel it is He who sends the wicked away to the place of outer darkness. This emphasis on Christ is surely a warning against any inclination to dismiss the divine anger as sub-Christian. But it is also a warning against describing the wrath itself in a way inconsistent with what we know of Jesus. There cannot be in the Wrath any un-Christlikeness at all.

The distinctive thing about the wrath to come is that it is unmitigated. In the present order, specific judgments are abbreviated for the sake of the elect (Matthew 24: 22), reprobate communities are spared for the sake of as few as ten righteous men (Genesis 18: 32) and the divine wrath is invariably mixed with blessing. Paul reminds us of this in the very context where he speaks of God's anger against his own civilisation: the riches of His kindness and forbearance and patience surround us even in the very midst of wrath, in order to lead us to repentance (Romans 2: 4).

But in the wrath to come, all modifiers and all limits and all mitigating factors are removed. The reprobate experience God's anger *simpliciter*, according to what their works deserve and the holy jealousy of God requires. This is symbolised in the parable of the Rich Man and Lazarus: not even a drop of cold water can be conceded (Luke 16: 24). Hell (according to the Lamb) is unmitigated torment. Paradoxically, the deepest insight we have into this is the experience of Christ Himself. He was not spared (Romans 8: 32). Instead, He was given absolutely, without limit or qualification (John 3: 16), to an experience which, in prospect, filled Him with chilled horror and astonishment and, in fulfillment, left Him bewildered and desolate.

Yet, in a way, there is a limit. The wrath is bounded by equity. God will not banish for the mere pleasure of it. He will banish only because it is right: and only to the extent that it is right. We can have an absolute confidence that God, the righteous judge, will take absolutely everything into account, including our excuses and any pleas we may have to offer in mitigation. Not one soul will be in Hell who does not deserve to be; and no one's Hell will be darker or deeper than is right. God's wrath cannot be compromised by miscarriages of justice. If we are sure that our lives are defensible, we have nothing to fear.

Outside

It is futile, not to say blasphemous, to speculate on the location and geography of hell. But there is one intriguing feature in the biblical references: a recurring emphasis on the idea of Hell being *outside*. Matthew, for example, reports the Lord as referring no fewer than three times to *outer* darkness (8: 12, 22: 13, 25: 30). John speaks of all those who love and practise falsehood being finally *outside* (Revelation 22: 15). There are corresponding ideas in the Old Testament, particularly in the instance of the scapegoat (Leviticus 16: 22), taken *outside* the camp to a wilderness without inhabitant. Some of the language used of Christ is also reminiscent of this. He is forsaken, absolutely, by God. He is crucified *outside* the gate. He comes to be *without* God (a variant reading of Hebrews 2: 9).

These are only hints, but it seems safe to move from them to the conclusion that Hell is *outside* the cosmos. The *cosmos* is the realm of order and beauty, the sphere within which law operates. Hell is no part of that. It has neither order nor beauty. It is Outside, the final Black Hole where the writ of Law and Logic do not run. It possesses neither moral nor physical order. It is simply a darkness which never has (and never can) hear the divine word, 'Let there be Light'. In this it corresponds to the essential nature of sin itself, defined by the Apostle John as *lawlessness* (1 John 3: 4). It admits of no explanation and knows no logic. It is simply an anomaly, its origin a mystery, the reasons for God's allowing it a mystery, its consequences utterly sterile. In the final reckoning, it is banished from the cosmos, thus ensuring a universe where the supremacy of Law is total and all Lawlessness is *outside*.

CHAPTER ELEVEN

WILL CHRISTIANS REJOICE IN THE WRATH?

In a famous sermon (*The End of the Wicked Contemplated by the Righteous*) Jonathan Edwards argued that 'when the saints in glory shall see the wrath of God executed on ungodly men, it will be no occasion of grief to them, but of rejoicing'. Edwards followed the logic of his own position remorselessly. Husbands and wives, brothers and sisters, will show no signs of sorrow when separated from their unbelieving kith and kin. Wicked men, 'who shall go to hell from under the labours of pious and faithful ministers, will see those ministers rejoicing and praising God upon the occasion of their destruction'. The saints 'will not be sorry for the damned; it will cause no uneasiness or dissatisfaction to them; but on the contrary, when they have this sight, it will excite them to joyful praises'.

Severely criticised

Not surprisingly, Edwards has been severely criticised. William Barclay, for example, wrote: 'It is very difficult to understand how those who claim to be disciples of the Lord who taught us to love and to forgive our enemies can anticipate the delight of seeing even the darkest sinner agonise in hell' (*The Plain Man Looks at the Apostles' Creed,* Collins, London 1967, p. 221).

But Edwards was by no means the only one to hold such a doctrine. Barclay himself quotes Tertullian as teaching that it would be part of the joy of heaven to see persecuting magistrates liquefying in fiercer flames than ever they kindled against the Christians. Thomas Aquinas wrote that the bliss of the saints will find its completion in the sight of the punishment of the wicked. Even the gentle Robert McCheyne preached a sermon entitled *The Eternal Torment of the Wicked, Matter of Eternal Song to the Redeemed* (*A Basket of Fragments,* Aberdeen, 1849, p. 324 ff).

Names such as these, along with that of Edwards, should be enough to warn us that this doctrine was not held lightly or unthinkingly.

We must remember, too, that in setting forth this idea

Edwards was actually expounding a text of Scripture: 'Rejoice over her, thou heaven, and ye holy apostles and prophets: for God hath avenged you on her' (Revelation 18: 20). These words certainly appear to support the notion that the saints will rejoice over the destruction of their persecutors.

Furthermore, McCheyne and Edwards both did their best to guard against misunderstanding. If the righteous rejoiced over the doom of the wicked it was not because they were sadists, delighting in the misery of others; and if they themselves preached this doctrine it was certainly not because they were morose bigots longing for revenge. Their position was well put by McCheyne: 'Oh! brethren, it is a solemn truth, and I know hardly how to speak of it; but as sure as there is a God in heaven, and as sure as there is a hell for the wicked, so surely will the redeemed rejoice over the eternal damnation of the wicked. *And this is the reason: We will enter into the same mind with God*' (*op. cit.*, p. 334). This is the crux of the matter. Edwards and McCheyne, Tertullian and Aquinas, were struggling with a problem which quickly carries us to the very frontiers of revelation: How can glorified saints be happy, knowing that millions of their fellow creatures are condemned eternally? They came up with the only possible answer: *the redeemed will have no mind but God's*. They will view the destruction of Satan and the condemnation of his seed not as partisans of creation but as partisans of the Creator. Those who judge no man after the flesh (2 Corinthians 5: 16) will not judge the Judgment after the flesh. They will rejoice in it as the vindication of God and as the assertion of His kingdom.

There is one more thing to say for Edwards. What was he trying to achieve by means of this sermon? Samuel T. Logan has recently argued that the concern underlying all Edwards' work was *to produce holy affections* and that this is a concern which all preachers must share: 'If what matters in ultimate terms is what one *really* loves or desires or fears, then the preacher speaking with the authority of his Lord must seek to create sermonic situations in which love for Christ *happens*, in which hatred for sin *happens*, in which desire for the blessing of God *happens*, in which fear of the consequences of sin *happens*. That is exactly how Edwards himself preached and his most famous sermon, *Sinners in the Hands of an Angry God* is a perfect example of the last of these' (*Preaching: the Preacher and Preaching in the Twentieth Century,* Evangelical Press, Welwyn 1986, p. 156ff). So, we might add, is the sermon we are now considering, *The End of the Wicked Contemplated by the Righteous*. Its stated object was to instil a saving fear in the hearts of men: 'I shall apply this subject only in one use, namely, of *warning* to ungodly men'. He wanted to confront men with the awful consequences of sin. Of course, this was only a prelude to presenting Christ. But it was a necessary prelude: one which God used mightily, and one which it would be arrogant for us, who have never known the kind of spiritual power experienced by Edwards, to dismiss.

Rejoicing in enmity against God?

But even if we agree that it was right to instil fear of the consequences of sin and right to use such a text as Revelation 18: 20 for this purpose, we can hardly endorse all that Edwards has to say. It is dangerous to translate the vivid imagery of *Revelation* into the cold prose of propositional theology. In John's vision, the saints rejoice over the destruction of an institution, the Roman Empire (portrayed as Babylon). And not only was it an institution: it was an institution of terrible ferocity. The feelings of the saints were such as we ourselves might experience at the collapse of Nazi Germany or the Soviet empire or the regime of Idi Amin. We have no right at all to assume that they reflect the way believers will react when they see individuals they have loved and cherished come under the condemnation of God.

We must remember, too, what it is we are being asked to rejoice in. Perdition is not only a state of grief and pain but a state of sin. It is a condition of endless rebellion, endless alienation and endless moral deterioration. God's judgment expressed within history on a political institution — that we can rejoice in. But the assignation of those we love to a state of eternal enmity against God is an entirely different matter and certainly not 'matter of praise to the redeemed'.

What must guide us in this whole area is, surely, the attitude of God Himself and that is described for us unmistakably in Ezekiel 33: 11: 'As I live, saith the Lord, I have no pleasure in the death of the wicked'. This makes it perfectly plain that God Himself is not excited to joyful praises by the destruction of the impenitent. We have already seen that however resolutely He condemns the defiant, His condemnation is rooted not in malice but in equity. He condemns only because it is right and even then we must believe (on the basis of Hosea 11: 8) that He acts with reluctance, not as one doing something He relishes but as one doing something He must.

What gives God no pleasure can give the Christian no pleasure either. He will rejoice over the conversion of a sinner and over any enlargement of the Kingdom of God. He will rejoice, too, over the vindication of Christ and the curtailment of evil. But he will surely experience no such feelings over the destruction of individual souls. Like God Himself, he is not willing that any should perish (2 Peter 3: 9): and the more Godlike he is the less will he be willing. He can no more enthuse over the loss of a soul than can God Himself. He can only say, as Christ Himself said in another connection, 'Even so, Father, for so it seemed good in thy sight' (Matthew 11: 26).

What can anyone say?

How can this be true and yet the Christian be blessed? How can he be happy when there is this thing in which he cannot rejoice?

But is this the real question? Is the real question not how *God* can be blessed while millions of His creatures are lost; or, deeper still, why He does not choose to overcome *all* human impenitence. We simply do not know. What we know is *Himself* (Job 42: 5): and that the Lamb is in the midst of His throne (Revelation 5: 6). He will do nothing that contradicts Himself. Even in His judgment there will be no un-Christlikeness at all.

'And with all this,' said Augustine, 'what have I said, my God and my Life and my sacred Delight? What can anyone say when he speaks of Thee? Yet woe to them that speak not of Thee at all, since those who say most are but dumb' (*Confessions*, I:IV).

CHAPTER TWELVE

THE GRACE THAT BRINGS SALVATION

In Christianity, someone has said, theology is grace and ethics is gratitude. Few who know the contours of biblical theology will quarrel with the assessment, least of all with its first part. The God of Scripture is pre-eminently a God of grace, no less in the Old Testament than in the New. In Exodus 34: 6, for example, He identifies Himself as 'the Lord, the Lord God, merciful and gracious'. In Christ, His eternal Word, He has declared Himself to be full of grace and truth (John 1: 14). His throne is a throne of grace (Hebrews 4: 16). In grace He elects. In grace He calls. By grace He saves. And for the glory of His grace the church exists.

The concept, then, is familiar enough. But what specific features of the divine character does it highlight? We can identify at least four different levels of meaning.

The gracefulness of God

First of all, Scripture uses the word *grace* in an aesthetic sense analogous to graceful. It bears this meaning as applied to a woman in Proverbs 11: 16, as applied to a doe in Proverbs 5: 19 and as applied to a precious stone (literally, 'a stone of grace') in Proverbs 17: 8. Similarly, when the community in Zechariah 4: 7 witness the laying of the foundation stone of the new temple they cry, 'Grace! Grace!' This can hardly refer to some quality of compassion in the stone. It indicates, rather, the people's delight in the beauty of the stone and, more especially, in the beauty of the project which it symbolised.

In Proverbs 22: 11 the idea of merely aesthetic beauty is close to merging in a moral one: 'He that loveth pureness of heart, for the grace of his lips the king shall be his friend'. In Psalm 45: 2 the transition has in fact taken place. The promised King is 'fairer than the children of men: grace is poured into thy lips: therefore God has blessed thee for ever'. In this passage, *to be fair* and *to be gracious* are synonymous. Psalm 27: 4 belongs to the same order of thought: 'One thing have I desired of the Lord: That I may dwell in the house of the Lord all the days of my life, to behold the beauty of the Lord'.

The aesthetic element is equally prominent in *charis*, the New Testament word for grace. Here the etymology itself is suggestive. *Charis* is derived from *chairein*, to rejoice, so that a person is gracious if he makes one rejoice or if he induces gladness. The usage confirms this. In Luke 4: 22, men wondered at the gracious words which proceeded from the lips of Jesus. In Colossians. 4: 6, Paul insists that the speech of Christians must be gracious, seasoned with salt. Peter applies the word to conduct which God may find beautiful or acceptable: 'If when you do well and suffer for it you take it patiently, this is acceptable (*charis*) with God' (1 Peter 2: 20). In John, grace is predicated specifically of the incarnate Saviour: 'We beheld his glory, the glory as of the only-begotten from the Father, full of grace and truth' (John 1: 14). Here again, the grace is something *beheld.* Far from contradicting His glory, it is synonymous with it; and as grace-glory it characterises Him even in His humiliation. His beauty appears in the way He dwelt among us.

In the revelation of the divine gracefulness, there is special emphasis on the *words* of God (Psalm 45: 2, Luke 4: 22). The effect of this is to relate His beauty in the closest possible way to the beauty of His message. At one level, of course, this arises from the fact that His words are about Himself. They are words of self-disclosure and hence as enthralling and fascinating as He is Himself. But equally there is a beauty in the specifically messianic message. He brings good news — a message of unspeakable hope and comfort, offering man peace and joy and strength. Even as such it remains a message about God and more particularly about His intention for man. Conversely, the idols are dumb, and when God Himself is silent — when the heavens are as brass and there is a famine of the word of the Lord — man loses confidence in His beauty.

There is an equal emphasis on the fact that this beauty is something to *behold* (Psalm 27: 4, John 1: 14). This is the supreme element in the Christian hope. The reward of the pure in heart is that they shall see God (Matthew 5: 8). Paul hopes to see Christ 'face to face' (1 Corinthians 13: 12) and John is confident that we shall see Him as He is (1 John 3: 2). These passages express not only a clear awareness of the captivatingness of God but also a measure of impatience with the vision and the access we enjoy at present. There is a longing to gaze uninterruptedly (Psalm 27: 4), confident that what we see will never either disappoint or weary us.

Paradoxically, the gracefulness of God has a very close connection with His holiness. The two qualities are explicitly linked more than once in the Psalms: 'Worship the Lord in the beauty of holiness' (29: 2): 'Oh! worship the Lord in the beauty of holiness' (96: 9). There is thus *prima facie* justification for Rudolf Otto's claim that the idea of the holy contains two separate values: not only the august, transcendent and intimidating but also the fascinating and the enthralling. Otto, of course, operates with virtually total indifference to the fact of man's spiritual blindness and native aversion to God. But where there has been spiritual renewal men not only fear God. They are drawn to Him — by the gracefulness of His words, by the graciousness of His glory and by the beauty of His holiness. He is love: and lovely.

To perceive this, and respond to it with our whole being, is the very core of Christian piety. Authentic religion, as Jonathan Edwards pointed out, consists very largely in holy affections and particularly in delighting in God: and 'the first foundation of the delight a true saint has in Christ is His own perfection; and the first foundation of the delight he has in Christ is His own beauty; He appears in Himself the chief among ten thousand and altogether lovely' (*Selected Works of Jonathan Edwards* , Vol III, The Banner of Truth Trust, London, 1961, p. 176). William Guthrie puts it even better: 'Now the heart is so enlarged for Him as that less cannot satisfy and more is not desired; the soul now resolves to die if He shall so command, yet at His door, and looking towards Him' (*The Christian's Great Interest*, Free Presbyterian Church of Scotland, 1951, p. 43).

'Let me see Thy face even if I die,' said Augustine, 'lest I die with longing to see it!'(*Confessions* I: V.).

A gracious disposition

The grace of God means, secondly, that He is of a gracious disposition. In saying this, we are not completely abandoning the primary idea already emphasised. His gracious disposition means that God finds others graceful (or treats them as if He did). The paradox is, of course, that the objects of His grace are sinners. Hence grace becomes characteristically not merely the disposition to show favour but the disposition to show favour to the undeserving. As such, it is the source of the whole work of redemption. God's salvation represents the very opposite of a movement prompted by regard to human merit as exemplified in works of moral or spiritual worth. It is a matter entirely of the donor's discretion. Its only constraint is the divine goodwill, a fact which is epitomisd in Paul's great summary explanation of his own calling: 'It pleased God!' (Galatians 1: 15).

Nor is man's undeservingness a merely preliminary factor in the background to his redemption. It persists up to the very moment of his receiving God's favour. Man is blind to his Maker's grace and fails to recognise it even when confronted by it. He hates it and turns away from it until grace itself overcomes his aversion to grace. And not only does God persist in His commitment of grace despite man's initial resistance. He also remains faithful in the face of our subsequent ingratitude and unfaithfulness. The words *grace* and *truth* (*emeth*, faithfulness) are frequently found in combination in the Old Testament (e.g. Psalm 85:10; 89:1; 100:5). The same combination is also found in John 1: 14, 'We beheld his glory, full of grace and truth'. To be in Christ is to be the object not only of God's gracious disposition, but also and equally of His fidelity.

This grace reigns through righteousness (Romans 5: 21). It holds the supremacy, but a supremacy bound up inextricably with the fact that Christ reigns. He is the fulness of grace — the incarnation of God's gracious disposition towards mankind. In His exaltation that disposition is placed, visibly, 'in the midst of the throne'. It holds all the initiatives. It has the right of final arbitration. It upholds, preserves and governs. It is invested, in Christ, with cosmic dominion and invincible might, enabling it to move irresistibly towards its goals.

But grace does not merely reign. It reigns through righteousness. Its interests are not secured at the expense of the divine integrity. On the contrary, it reigns unto forgiveness only because, prior to justification, God set forth His Son as a propitiation declaring His righteousness. Similarly, grace reigns in the moral life of the believer only because Christ, by paying the price of redemption, has established His own ownership of the soul. Equally, grace reigns over the universe only because Christ, the incarnation of grace, has earned His supremacy by His obedience unto Death (Philippians 2: 9). Hence the unchallengeableness of the sovereignty of grace, resting not on the fluctuating moral performance of men or on the whim of a sentimental and amoral deity but on the obedience of the grace-bearer, Jesus Christ, glorified because He finished the work which God gave Him to do (John 17: 4).

Grace, therefore, although free, is not cheap and as Karl Barth points out, this has important consequences for the way we should respond to it: 'It cost God dear enough to give this answer, to send His Son as the Saviour of the world. Therefore, if our answer is to correspond to His, if it is to have weight and meaning, it cannot be a cheap or over-hasty answer' (*Church Dogmatics* , Volume IV, Part 1, p. 216).

'I beseech you, therefore, brethren, by the mercies of God, that ye present your bodies a living sacrifice, holy, acceptable unto God, which is your reasonable service' (Romans 12: 1).

The power which actually saves

We have already hinted at the third shade of meaning involved in the concept of grace: the power which actually saves the sinner. Historically, this was specially emphasised in the Anti-Pelagian treatises of Augustine. 'This grace is rejected by no hard heart,' he writes, 'because it is given for the sake of first taking away the hardness of the heart' (*On the Predestination of the Saints*, Chap. 13). 'The grace by which strength is perfected in all weakness,' he says again, 'actually conducts all who are called and predestinated to the highest perfection and glory. By such grace it is effected not only that we discover what ought to be done, but also that we do what we discover' (*On the Grace of Christ*, Chap. 13). He expresses himself most graphically, however, in the famous prayer, 'Give what Thou dost command and command what Thou wilt!' (*Confessions*, X: XXIX)

J.H. Jowett, a great preacher of 80 years ago, crystallised the Augustinian doctrine in a sermon entitled *The Energy of Grace*: 'Grace is too commonly regarded as a pleasing sentiment, a soft disposition, a welcome feeling of cosy favour entertained toward us by our God. The interpretation is ineffective, and inevitably cripples the life in which it prevails. Grace is more than a smile of good nature. It is not the shimmering face of an illumined lake; it is the sunlit majesty of an advancing sea. It is a transcendent and ineffable force, *the outgoing energies of the redeeming personality of God washing against the polluted shores of human need*' (*Apostolic Optimism and Other Sermons*, London, 1901, p. 113).

This view of grace as the forth-putting of God's redemptive energy is thoroughly biblical. In Titus 2: 11, for example, Paul speaks of the grace of God as 'bringing salvation'. The word underlying the English version is the adjective *soterios*, meaning literally 'salvation-bearing': 'there has been an epiphany of the salvation-bearing grace of God'. Grace not only desires salvation. It confers it. II Corinthians 12: 9 points even more clearly in the same direction: 'My grace is sufficient for thee: for My strength is made perfect in weakness. Most gladly, therefore, will I rather glory in my infirmities, that the power of Christ may rest upon me'. Here, grace is the answer to human weakness; it is synonymous with the strength of God and the power of Christ; and it is sufficient for all the exigencies of our human situation. In the words of Hebrews 4: 16, grace is God's help in times of need.

It is from this point of view that grace is *irresistible*: not in the sense that men cannot resist it but in the old Latin sense that it carries all before it. It is invincible because it flows out of God's determination to save and represents the commitment of all God's resources to that end. It is, to return to Jowett's phraseology, the redemptive might of an omnipotent God pounding upon the shores of human need. It takes away sin. It liberates. It enlightens. It transfigures. It enables us to overcome temptations, to bear burdens, to endure suffering. Through it we are more than conquerors, and, even in the most inauspicious circumstances, mount up on wings, as eagles, run and are not weary, walk and do not faint (Isaiah 40: 31).

The source of the charismata

Finally, grace is the source of gifts for ministry. The *charismata* are rooted in *charis* (grace). Whatever our views as to the cessation of some of the gifts of the apostolic period the church is perennially, and of necessity, a charismatic community. It cannot be sustained by any aggregate of natural gifts, however splendid. It depends on a constant supply of God-given officers and servants endowed with the charismata necessary for their particular functions. Without these gifts there is no divine call to service and no divine authority for the church to ordain. Not even the highest academic and professional competence can compensate for the lack of these. Nor can the severest shortage of manpower justify our laying hands on ungifted men in the hope that God will some day supply them with what He has so far withheld.

These charismata are for the benefit of the whole body of Christ, not for the glory of individuals: 'He gave some apostles; some prophets; some evangelists; and some pastors and teachers; for the perfecting of the saints, for the edifying of the body of Christ' (Ephesians 4: 12ff.). The objectives of such a ministry are largely qualitative — to create a mature, stable, intelligent, diligent and loving community of believers. But it is also the function of a biblical, charismatic ministry to promote the quantitative growth of the church through missionary endeavour. Sadly, the evangelistic, church-planting gifts are the rarest in the church today, although we may well question whether this is due not to the sovereignty of God in withholding them but to the structures of the church in discouraging and stifling them.

Christ distributes these gifts among the whole membership of the church. No member of His body is useless, nor can any say to another, 'I have no need of you' (I Corinthians 12: 21). The church is a community of mutually dependent individuals, each contributing to the common weal. This was the basic perspective of Pentecost: the whole community exists in order to show forth the wonderful works of God (Acts 2: 11); and precisely because of that, each disciple must receive power (Acts 1: 8). For too long, in all the traditional denominations, too much has been left to the ministry of one man, the pastor. Recent years have seen a significant increase in lay participation. But the process has a long way to go before we have a situation where every member of the congregation not only draws from the body but also contributes to it according to his own particular charisma.

It is God, of course, who must in the last analysis nourish and sustain His own gifts. But this cannot justify mere passivity on our part. We must be careful not to quench the Spirit or to despise His gifts. Instead, we must stir up the gift of God that is in us (2 Timothy 1: 6), not suppressing or undervaluing it, but fanning it into flame. We must nourish and cultivate it. We must exercise it, boldly yet meekly, forgetful of the envy of others, heedless of the charge of pride which is often the lot of those who attempt to do anything, lost in concern for the glory of Christ and the good of His body, the church.

CHAPTER THIRTEEN

COMMON GRACE

Alongside the doctrine of redemptive grace, Reformed theology also developed the doctrine of Common Grace. This was intended to account especially for three factors in the human situation.

First, the blessings enjoyed by the reprobate. The sun shines on them, the rain falls, their harvests are plentiful and their prosperity often far exceeds that of the righteous.

Secondly, the laudable qualities to be found in the lives of those who are totally alienated from God. They are often exemplary citizens, courageous patriots, wise and affectionate parents. Their lives are usually decent and sometimes even heroic.

Thirdly, the cultural achievements of the natural man. He has toiled with conspicuous success in the fields of art, literature, music, philosophy, politics, medicine, engineering and indeed in every area of human endeavour.

Against this background, Reformed theology, deriving from Calvin (*Institutes II*: III, 4), developed the doctrine of Common Grace. Recognising that under the guidance of nature there have in every age been men who devoted themselves to virtue, Calvin comments: 'Those are not common endowments of nature, but special gifts of God, which He distributes in diverse forms, and in a definite measure to men otherwise profane' (*Institutes II*: III, 3). He also recognises a general divine restraint placed upon human depravity: 'We ought to consider that, notwithstanding the corruption of our nature, there is room for divine grace, such grace as, without purifying it, may lay it under internal restraint' (op. cit., *II*:III, 3). Later Reformed theology spoke with the same voice. Abraham Kuyper, for example, wrote: 'There is a particular grace which works salvation, and also a common grace by which God, maintaining the life of the world, relaxes the curse which rests upon it, arrests its process of corruption, and thus allows the untrammelled development of our life in which to glorify Himself as Creator' (*Lectures on Calvinism,* Erdmans, Grand Rapids, 1961, p.30). All the blessings enjoyed by the reprobate, all their laudable qualities and all their achievements derive ultimately from this source.

Distinguished from Special Grace

Common grace is distinguished in several important respects from special redemptive grace.

First, whereas special grace embraces only the elect, common grace embraces all men. God confers blessings and imposes restraints on the unrighteous as well as the righteous, the evil as well as the good.

Secondly, common grace is not redemptively effective. As Calvin recognises, while it restrains it does not purify. The level of divine activity is not such as to lead to reconciliation or regeneration or real holiness.

Thirdly, common grace is set within the framework of special grace. The fact that God's redemptive purpose embraces only the elect must not blind us to the fact that, cosmically, the redemptive purpose is central. God's core commitment is to salvation and His administration of the universe has constant regard to this. This is implied in the fact that Christ is on the cosmic throne (Revelation 5: 6) and expressed in Paul's assertion that all things are ours (1 Corinthians 3: 22). The civilising and restraining effects of common grace are always subordinated to God's determination to create a community for His firstborn (Romans 8: 29).

Effects of Common Grace

The primary effect of common grace is that God exercises forbearance and longsuffering towards the world. Man collectively deserves the judicial outpouring of divine wrath. But God suspends it. This truth is clearly expressed in the New Testament. For example, Paul (Romans 2: 4) speaks of the riches of God's goodness, forbearance and longsuffering, persevering even in the face of hardened impenitence. He speaks to similar effect in Romans 9: 22, referring especially to God enduring with much longsuffering the vessels of wrath fitted to destruction. Nor is the doctrine confined to Paul. Peter is equally articulate, speaking of the longsuffering of God 'waiting' in the days of Noah (1 Peter 3: 20). This longsuffering is not only negative. Paul speaks of its 'riches' and Peter says we should esteem it salvation (II Peter 3: 15). It expresses that reality in the heart of God of which Paul speaks in 1 Timothy 2: 4, 'God our Saviour will have all men to be saved'.

But common grace also means that man universally receives the blessings of the divine benevolence. In fact this was often a problem to the writers of the Old Testament, especially from the point of view that the godless seemed to prosper more than the godly. The Preacher complains that one thing happens to the evil and to the good (Ecclesiastes 9: 2). Asaph found the problem 'too painful' (Psalm 73: 1-17). The wicked were not plagued or troubled. They increased in riches until they had more than they could wish. David, similarly, saw the wicked accumulating great wealth and power (Psalm 37: 5). Whatever questions the prosperity of the ungodly may suggest as to God's administration of the world, it does at least indicate that God does not deal with defiant man as he deserves but grants him many blessings, even to the extent that the prosperity of His enemies causes His people to ask whether God knows what He is doing (Psalm 73: 11).

Another of the effects of common grace is that God places restraints upon sin. This applies also, of course, within the sphere of special grace. David prays to be kept back from presumptuous sin (Psalm19: 13). But it is especially conspicuous in God's general government of the world. God sets bounds to man's violence and confines his corruption so that life does not become impossible and society does not collapse. Men do not become devils, earth does not become Hell, and sin does not fully accomplish its destructive work. 'Did the Lord let every mind loose to wanton in its lusts,' wrote Calvin, 'doubtless there is not a man who would not show that his nature is capable of all the crimes with which God charges it' (*op. cit.*, II: III, 3).

Through common grace God also preserves some sense of morality and religion in human society. The Gentiles show by their behaviour that they have the law written on their hearts (Romans 2: 14). Those who have no vital relationship with God are still capable of moral indignation, religious decorum, respect for the people of God, and even diligent use of the means of grace. It was the perception of these facts that led the Synod of Dordt to embody in its Canons (III: IV; 4) the statement: 'There remain, however, in man since the Fall, the glimmerings of natural light, whereby he retains some knowledge of God, of natural things and of the difference between good and evil, and shows some regard for virtue and for good outward behaviour.' They were careful to add, however: 'So far is this light of nature from being sufficient to bring him to a saving knowledge of God and true conversion that he is incapable of using it aright even in things natural and civil.'

Yet another effect of common grace is that fallen man

remains capable of both civil good and domestic affection. Those who totally reject the gospel are frequently exemplary citizens, obeying the powers that be, quick to serve and defend their countries and exemplifying a high degree of patriotism. The same is true in the domestic sphere. Family love (*storge*) is not confined to the regenerate. Natural men provide for their own faithfully and sometimes even heroically. Only a civilisation that is hopelessly reprobate can be described as 'without natural affection' (Romans 1: 31).

Cultural and technological achievement, equally, is a product of divine grace. By God's mandate and with His blessing, man has made gigantic strides in medical research, in understanding and exploiting his environment and in probing the complexities of micro-cellular and sub-atomic existence. 'If the Lord has been pleased to assist us by the work and ministry of the ungodly in physics, dialectics, mathematics and other similar sciences,' wrote Calvin, 'let us avail ourselves of it, lest by neglecting the gifts of God spontaneously offered to us, we be justly punished for our sloth' (*op. cit.*, II: II, 16). Christians such as Copernicus, Galileo, Newton, Boyle and James Young Simpson, have made outstanding contributions to the advancement of science. But others who professed no allegiance to the Kingdom of God have made equally important contributions. 'The one Aristotle knew more of the cosmos than all the Church Fathers taken together,' wrote Abraham Kuyper, 'and under the dominion of Islam, better cosmic science flourished than in the cathedral and monastic schools of Europe' (*op. cit.*, p. 117). The achievements of unbelieving scientists reflect the goodness of God not only towards the scientists on whom He conferred splendid endowments but also towards the race which enjoys the benefits of their discoveries.

The same is true in the realm of art, as appears clearly in Exodus 31: 1-11. Bezaleel is filled with the Spirit of God specifically for the purpose of skilled craftwork in gold, silver, brass, gems and timber. Aholiab is similarly endowed and the Tabernacle is the result of their joint skills. These men may very well have been regenerate. At least they belonged to the visible people of God. But others, not regenerate, have possessed similar skills in painting, sculpture, architecture, music, poetry and so on, reflecting the creativity of God and modifying the satanic degeneration of the world into ugliness and despair.

The Instruments of Common Grace

The primary instrument of common grace is God's general revelation. Even with regard to pagans, God has not left Himself without witness (Acts 14: 17). In the glories of creation, the events of providence and the instincts and data of the human consciousness, He has made visible His invisible qualities (Romans 1 :20). He has even written His Law on men's hearts. Furthermore, man is so made that he sees the revelation clearly (Romans 1: 20). He deduces from it God's eternal power, wisdom, love and integrity. He knows himself to be obligated by divine law and answerable to God (Romans 1: 32). Sadly, he is not led to worship God or to be thankful. But he does, nevertheless, live under the régime of conscience (Romans 2: 15), so that he is aware not only of what he is doing but of what his action deserves. Even where there is no gospel and no spiritual enlightenment there are those things which 'nature teaches', so that even specifically secular states and avowedly atheistic societies still possess strong ethical structures.

The presence of the church in the world is another instrument of common grace. At one level, the Christian community has an exemplary and illuminative function. It is a light in the world's darkness, exposing impurity and duplicity, illuminating the true moral and spiritual potential of man and spreading truth and optimism. At another level, Christians, individually and collectively, simply by being what they are, restrain and inhibit the depravity, dissoluteness and selfishness of the world around them. They are the salt of the earth (Matthew 5: 13). It is also true that the presence of a group of believers within a particular society can secure for it the special favour of God, or at least the mitigation of a judgment which it fully deserves. God conceded to Abraham that if there had been ten righteous persons in Sodom He would not have destroyed it 'for ten's sake'. Similarly, Christ concedes that the great tribulation will be shortened 'for the elect's sake' (Matthew 24: 22).

God also uses the ordinances of law and government as instruments of His common grace. He instituted political power with the specific intention that it should be a terror to the workers of evil and to this end authorised it to enact laws and to enforce them with appropriate sanctions — ultimately with the sword (Romans 13: 4). The importance of such restrictive legislation should not be underestimated. Sadly, this is the only language some men understand: 'It is the hangman that hinders me from sinning,' said Luther, 'as chains, ropes and strong bands hinder bears, lions and other wild beasts from tearing and rending in pieces all that come in their way' (*Table Talk*, CCLXXIV). 'God has ordained magistrates, elders, schoolmasters, laws and statutes', he says again, 'to the end, if they can do no more, that at least they may bind the claws of the Devil and hinder him from raging and swelling so powerfully in those who are his' (*op. cit.* CCLXXIV). Calvin made a similar assessment, laying down that the second use of the law was 'by means of its fearful denunciations and the consequent dread of punishment, to curb those who, unless forced, have no regard for rectitude and justice. Such persons are curbed, not because their mind is inwardly moved and affected, but because, as if a bridle were laid upon them, they restrained them from external acts, and internally checked the depravity which would otherwise petulantly break forth' (*Institutes* II:VII, 10).

Yet this negative side of government responsibility is not all. Government is also bound before God to create a framework within which men can live lives of peace and decency, honour and godliness. This implies that it is God's will for man, in common grace, that 'the powers that be' should respect and promote human rights and do all in their power to create an economic, social and physical environment in which men can achieve the highest development which their fallenness allows. It naturally follows that the charismata appropriate to political leadership are within God's gift and that any community which feels itself bereft of them should offer urgent supplication to the great Font of all wisdom, vision and courage.

Closely associated with this is the influence of public opinion. Every society has its own moral consensus, sometimes reflecting little more than the concern for communal survival, at other times approximating remarkably closely to the revealed ethic of Christianity. Whatever the level of its insight, it can be a considerable force, using the fear of discovery and the possibility of public disapproval and ostracism to secure conformity with its own standards. The result can be a significant curtailment of many kinds of immoral behaviour, ranging from promiscuity and infidelity to racial discrimination and indolence. Sadly, the alarming world-wide drift to the cities which is so striking a feature of twentieth century life looks set to rob this principle of much of its effectiveness. Urban life gives a considerable degree of anonymity and greatly increases the possibility of a Jekyll and Hyde existence on the part of even the most honourable citizens. Finding a proper balance between an appropriate privacy and a demoralising facelessness will tax man's wisdom to the limit.

Yet another instrument of common grace is the pattern of God's providential dealings with mankind. In biblical times, God frequently 'visited the earth' in judgment. The flood, the destruction of Sodom and Gomorrah and the virtual extermination of the Canaanites are outstanding instances of this principle. These were not only exemplary interventions, serving as deterrents to others. They were surgical operations, removing moral malignancies which because of their strategic relation to our cultural blood-stream threatened the whole course of civilisation. Such operations did not end with biblical times. God has repeatedly erupted into history since then, revealing His wrath againt successive civilisations which have resisted and perverted the truth. The Roman, Spanish and French empires have all come under His judgment. More recently, Tsarism and Nazism suffered the same fate. The civilisations of today are no less arrogant in their pretensions and some deny human rights with a ferocity never surpassed in the sad history of man's inhumanity to man. For the moment, they seem invulnerable, protected from subversion by the activities of secret police and from external assault by their nuclear umbrellas. But their day will come, as will that of the permissive and anarchical societies of the west: 'For the nation and kingdom that will not serve thee shall perish; yea, those nations shall be utterly wasted' (Isaiah 60: 12).

Finally, common grace operates through the external call of the gospel. Some who never truly come to Christ are nevertheless 'called by the ministry of the Word and may have some common operations of the Spirit' (*Westminster Confession* X: IV). Our Lord Himself made clear reference to this fact: 'Many are called but few are chosen' (Matthew 22: 14). Such a call acquaints men with the central realities of the gospel. They learn of the goodness and severity of God, of the lordship, sacrifice and resurrection of Christ, of justification by faith alone, of eternal life and of the need to be born again. They are invited — and even pleaded with (2 Corinthians 5: 20) — to come to Christ. Nor is the effect merely intellectual. They may be 'pricked in their hearts' (Acts 2: 37). They may, like Felix, tremble (Acts 24: 25). They may receive the Word with joy and for a time live such outwardly changed lives that they are indistinguishable from genuine disciples (Mark 4: 16ff). They may even be so affected as to reflect the condition described in Hebrews 6: 4 f.: they are enlightened, they partake of the Holy Spirit and of the powers of the world to come; they even taste the goodness of the Word of God. In the last analysis, admittedly, the spiritual effect of all this is deleterious. Men become hardened, ' even under those means which God useth for the softening of others' (*Westminster Confession* V: VI). But this in no way rules out the corresponding truth that such exposure to the gospel has a restraining effect on men and often leads to considerable reformation and elevation of men's lifestyle, both individually and communally.

CHAPTER FOURTEEN

OBJECTIONS TO COMMON GRACE

The doctrine of common grace has not gone unchallenged, however. There have been strident voices of protest even from within Reformed theology itself. The most emphatic has been that of Hermann Hoeksema, who has argued (*Reformed Dogmatics*, Grand Rapids, 1973, *passim*) that the position represented by his fellow Dutch theologians, Kuyper, Bavinck, Berkhof and Van Til, opens the door to Arminianism and Pelagianism.

Favourable disposition to lost sinners?

It is objected, first of all, that the idea of common grace presupposes a favourable disposition on God's part to lost sinners and that this is inconsistent with biblical teaching. The problem with this is that Scripture itself clearly indicates such an attitude. In Matthew 5: 44ff, for example, we are told to love our enemies for the precise reason that God loves His, and sends His sun to shine on the righteous and on the unrighteous. In the parallel passage in Luke (6: 35ff) God is said to be kind (*chrestos*) to the unthankful and to the wicked and upon this fact the Lord bases the directive that His disciples are to show pity or mercy (*oikturmos*) to those who hate them. To the same effect, Paul proclaims in Acts 14: 17 that God's 'doing good' embraces all those to whom He sends rain from heaven and fruitful seasons, thereby filling their hearts with food and gladness. In fact, the doctrine is rooted in the Old Testament, which assures us that, 'The Lord is good to all and his tender mercies extend to all that he has made' (Psalm 145: 9). Psalm 36 goes even further, rejoicing that God's mercy is in the heavens, that His faithfulness reaches even to the clouds and that Jehovah exercises these attributes in preserving man and beast (Psalm 36: 5f). Nor is the discovery original to the Psalmist. He is only reflecting the teaching of Genesis 9: 8ff, where, referring to the covenant of preservation, God says to Noah, 'And I, behold, I establish my covenant with you, and with your seed after you; and with every living creature that is with you, of the fowl, of the cattle, and of every beast of the earth with you.' What emerges from all these passages is, surely, that 'unregenerate men are recipients of divine favour and goodness' (John Murray, *Collected Writings*, The Banner of Truth Trust, Edinburgh, 1977, Vol II. p 109). They may be hostile and condemned, yet God is spoken of as loving them, being kind to them, being merciful to them and blessing them with gifts of inestimable value.

As a corollary to this, it should be borne in mind that just as the reprobate can be spoken of as in some sense objects of God's favour, so the elect themselves can be spoken of as in some sense objects of His disfavour. His attitude to them is not simply one of love. Before they come to be justified through faith in Christ, they are children of wrath, just like others (Ephesians 2: 3). By nature they are under divine condemnation and have to be reconciled by the death of Christ. Nor is it only in their pre-justification state that believers are objects simultaneously of God's favour and disfavour. It is precisely those whom He loves that God reproves and chastens (Revelation 3: 19). It is the legitimate children, not the illegitimate, who are scourged (Hebrews 12: 7f). We are told that the anger of the Lord was kindled against Israel (2 Samuel 24: 1) and find repeatedly that it is towards them, not the Gentiles, that both God's wrath and His longsuffering are directed. Berkhof quite rightly concludes: 'If they who are the objects of God's restoring love can also in some sense of the word be regarded as objects of His wrath, why should it be impossible that they who are the objects of His wrath should also in some sense share His divine favour?' (*Systematic Theology*, The Banner of Truth Trust, London, 1959, p. 445).

The accursedness of creation

A second objection to the doctrine of common grace is that it is inconsistent with the accursedness of creation. According to this point of view, the world is exclusively evil and horrible and Christians can have no part in it. The only course open to them is to separate from it, create their own self-contained communities and leave secular art, politics, culture and commerce to the children of darkness.

But the very problem to which the concept of common grace is proposed as a solution is that there are praiseworthy things in the world and this objection amounts only to cutting the knot. It ignores, for example, the result of the Christian presence in society, 'Ye are the light of the world, ye are the salt of the earth'. Because of this presence, all is not rottenness. 'The church of the Redeemer,' writes G.G. Findlay, 'has not toiled and suffered through these centuries without raising the moral standard and softening the temper of civilised mankind' (*Fellowship in the Life Eternal*, Hodder and Stoughton, London 1909, p. 198). It also ignores Paul's recognition in Philippians 4: 8ff that there are things of good report outside the sphere of grace (it is highly significant that many of the terms that Paul uses in this passage are technical terms of pagan philosophy, seldom used elsewhere in the New Testament). Above all, this perspective ignores the fact that to equate the present with the worst of all possible worlds is to minimise the distinction between earth and hell. It is true of all men, on this side of the judgment, that 'God hath not dealt with us after our sins; nor rewarded us according to our iniquities' (Psalm 103: 10). No spot in God's universe is yet so forsaken that it can be equated with hell. By the ordinance of God, evil is restrained, righteousness is rewarded (Romans 13: 3) and it is still possible for men to live quiet and peaceable lives in all godliness and honour (1 Timothy 2: 2). In recognition of this, the Lord specifically concedes that His people are not to be taken out of the world but only kept from its evil (John 17: 15). He Himself was fully involved, beyond any necessity of business or even evangelism, attending a wedding at Cana and indeed socialising to such an extent as to lay Himself open to the charge of being a 'winebibber' and the friend of publicans and sinners. It is in that very world — in the midst of 'a wicked and perverse nation' — that we are to hold forth the word of life (Philippians 2: 15, 16). Indeed, Paul recognises that complete separation from the world is physically impossible for the Christian: he can forbid us to keep company with Christian brethren who are fornicators but he cannot extend his ban to fornicators in general, or the covetous or extortioners or idolators, 'for then you would need to go out of the world altogether' (1 Corinthians 5: 10).

Inconsistent with total depravity

The third objection is that the notion of common grace is inconsistent with the doctrine of man's total depravity. According to both Scripture and confessional theology every function of human personality is affected by sin. We are incapable of attaining to the biblical standard of love. Our perception of facts is distorted and the inferences we make from them often perverse. Our emotions are disordered. Our wills are enslaved to selfishness, worldliness and godlessness. The light of conscience is often darkness. Even our bodies are affected — we have enlisted them in the service of unrighteousness (Romans 6: 13). The result of this pervasive depravity is that we are dead in sin (Ephesians 2:1), in enmity against God and quite unable to keep His law (Romans 8: 7). We see no beauty in Christ (Isaiah 53: 2) and cannot receive the things of the Spirit of God (1 Corinthians 2: 14). Collating these biblical passages we arrive at the conclusion that man 'has lost all ability of will to any spiritual good accompanying salvation' (*Westminster Confession* IX.III). The *Shorter Catechism* expresses the same doctrine less technically: 'No mere man since the fall is able in this life perfectly to keep the commandments of God, but doth daily break them in thought, word and deed' (Answer 82).

It would be easy enough to show that the theologians who have most vigorously advocated the doctrine of common grace have also accepted unreservedly the above assessment of human nature. But they distinguished between total depravity ('wholly defiled in all the faculties and parts of soul and body', *Westminster Confession*, VI.III) and absolute depravity. Hoeksema is well aware of the distinction (*Reformed Dogmatics*, p. 252) but denies that it can give any help to the exponents of the idea of common grace. It is difficult to follow him in this. Absolute depravity means such a degree of hostility to God as admits of no progression or variation. This is not the way the Bible portrays man. Human beings are not devils. Nor is any man so advanced in evil that he could not possibly become worse. Nor again does human society present a uniform level of degradation and depravity. It would be absurd to minimise, let alone deny, the difference between Hitler and Gandhi, Pharaoh and George Washington, Judas Iscariot and Pilate's wife. It would be equally absurd to maintain that Romans 1: 18-32 gives an accurate description of human society in every age and every place. The theology of the Reformation was well aware that 'some sins in themselves, and by reason of several aggravations, are more heinous in the sight of God than others' (*Shorter Catechism*, Answer 83). To conceive of all men as standing together on a flat, undifferentiated moral plateau is to exclude from theology altogether the doctrine of judicial abandonment. All men are depraved. But not all men are 'hardened' or 'given over to a reprobate mind'. Not every prison is an Auschwitz or every city a Sodom. Many men are capable of natural affection, fidelity and even of heroic self-sacrifice. The doctrine of common grace recognises this and insists that such qualities are gifts from 'the Father of lights' (James 1: 17).

Man never does good

The fourth objection is that man never does good; and that the Bible says so quite literally: 'There is none that does good, no, not one (Romans 3: 12, quoting Psalm 14: 1,3).

The range of such statements needs to be carefully defined, however. Man is incapable of spiritual good — of any moral achievement which can serve either as a ground or a preparation for salvation (*Westminster Confession*, IX.III). He is incapable of obeying the law of God: that is, he cannot love God with all his heart, nor can he love his neighbour as he loves himself. Or, changing the perspective once more, he is incapable, constitutionally and ontologically, of turning to God in repentance and faith.

But the unregenerate man may still be capable of works which, 'for the matter of them, may be things which God commands, and of good use both to themselves and others' (*Westminster Confession*, XVI.VII). As we have already seen, Paul indicates in Philippians 4: 8ff that there exist, even outside the sphere of redemption, things which are true, righteous, honourable, praiseworthy and virtuous and which deserve the support of the Christian in his function as the salt of the earth and the light of the world. He also indicates in Romans 2: 14 that the Gentiles, at least occasionally, do the things contained in the law; and further, that there are things which nature itself teaches (1 Corinthians 11: 14) and with which ordinary people, out of a sense of decency, comply. In accordance with this, a Roman centurion is commended because 'he loves our nation and built us a synagogue' (Luke 7: 5); the Jews at Berea are praised as being 'more noble' than those at Thessalonica (Acts 17: 11); and some slave-owners are distinguished from others as being 'good and gentle' (1 Peter 2: 18). It was surely 'good' of Darius the Mede to set Daniel over all his other administrators because 'an excellent spirit was in him' (Daniel 6: 3).

If we define *the good* as perfect conformity of thought, word and deed, of motive and emotion, to the law of God, then no man is good. But if we allow that, without forgetting this higher meaning, we may also define *the good* quite biblically as doing what nature teaches, showing natural affection and manifesting respect for life, property and marriage, for duly constituted authority and for the ordinances of the church, then we may distinguish some unregenerate men from others as *good*: and go on to explain the difference as a gift of God, expressing His common grace.

Grace which doesn't save

The fifth objection is that grace cannot be grace unless it is saving.

The first point to be made in answer to this is that the Bible itself does not limit the meaning of the word *grace* in this way. For example, Christ received grace (Luke 2: 40) and it certainly could not have been, in His case, redemptive. Furthermore, the New Testament clearly speaks of God *loving* some whom He does not save — such as the unrighteous on whom He makes His sun to shine and His rain to fall (Matthew 5: 45). We should also bear in mind the close connection between *charis* (grace) and *charisma* (gift). It would obviously be absurd to argue that no gift is a gift unless it is saving: as if the Queen could never be said to show favour or bestow a gift unless she gave away the kingdom (or laid down her life). There is 'an unspeakable gift' (2 Corinthians 9: 15). But it is not the only gift or the only evidence of divine favour.

We are warranted, then, in concluding that there may be love, grace and gift even where God's favour does not go the length of invincibly opening hearts and making them receptive to the gospel.

It is only a different form of the same objection when some scholars argue that the preaching of the gospel is not grace for the lost since it is not accompanied by regeneration and spiritual illumination. Again, the objection is more logical than scriptural. It was an advantage to the Jew that he had the oracles of God, whatever his personal response to them (Romans 3: 1f). The Christian presence is salt and light in any community and the benefits it brings are felt not only by the saved but by the unsaved. Even where there is no personal experience of salvation many people enjoy considerable political, social, educational, cultural and medical privileges which are the direct result of the gospel's influence on civilisation.

Furthermore, if we were to pursue this objection to its logical conclusion we should have to argue that since preaching the gospel gives men an opportunity to refuse it and thereby increase their guilt it would be infinitely better if they did not hear it at all. For many (on this view) evangelism only creates the possibility of a deeper and darker hell. The biblical view, by contrast, is that the sending of preachers is an expression of God's desire that all men should be saved; and that it puts men in a position of hope by placing the possibility of faith and salvation within their grasp. Indeed, it is the very fact that hearing the gospel is a privilege that makes rejection of it so heinous. If it were not a privilege, but a callous test which they were bound to fail, then evangelised unbelievers would have to be pitied, not condemned. To blame them is to recognise that they enjoyed the inestimable blessing of having Christ and His salvation sincerely and even earnestly offered to them and, on their own recognisance, rejected Him.

Unbiblical dualism

The next objection, urged particularly by Hoeksema, is that the doctrine of common grace presupposes an unbiblical dualism: 'It proceeds from the erroneous assumption that sin, death and the curse, instead of being powers which God works, manifestations of His wrath, are powers outside Him and apart from Him, which He must restrain' (*op. cit.*, p. 236). It is of course true that sin, death and the curse are not powers that operate apart from God. But it is hardly a satisfactory alternative to suggest that they are powers which God works. They are abstractions or personifications. Speaking precisely, God restrains not sin and death but the moral agents — men and devils — responsible for them. Dualism of this kind, positing the existence of real agencies other than God — and especially evil agencies — is thoroughly biblical. To eliminate the distinction between God and the Devil is to land in a thorough-going monism, making God not only the First Cause of all but the Only Cause. From a Christian point of view this is quite unacceptable; and, when it goes the length of regarding sin as something which 'God works', virtually blasphemous. Heaven and hell are distinct, although utterly unequal, empires. Eventually, heaven will be completely triumphant. For the moment, the divine will is to restrain evil — a fact which is graphically portrayed in Revelation Twenty where Satan is bound with a great chain and thrown into a bottomless pit which is then locked and sealed.

Unnecessary

One last objection deserves a brief notice: the doctrine of

common grace is unnecessary because the good things in human society can be explained quite adequately by the organic connection between good and evil men. 'There proceeds out of the eternal good pleasure of God in Christ,' writes Hoeksema, 'an operation of grace upon the elect kernel of our race, *in connection with the organic whole of all creatures*. And by that wonder of grace that elect kernel in Christ, *always in connection with the whole of things*, is redeemed, saved, liberated, glorified' (*op. cit.*, p. 744). On this view, evil men receive blessings not because of common grace — not because of any gracious disposition on God's part towards them — but because they are so closely connected with the people of God, socially and organically, that God cannot bless the one group without blessing the other. The tares are blessed only because they are inextricably mixed up with the wheat.

The organic connection between good men and evil men is of course indisputable. But it is difficult to see any conflict between this and the doctrine of common grace. It was as much God's intention that crumbs should fall to the pagan as that His own children should be richly provided for. 'Many blessings,' wrote William Cunningham, 'flow to mankind at large from the death of Christ, collaterally and incidentally, in consequence of the relation in which men, viewed collectively, stand to each other. All these benefits were, of course, foreseen by God, when He resolved to send His Son into the world; they were contemplated or designed by Him as what men should receive and enjoy; and they are to be viewed as coming to men through the channel of Christ's mediation' (*Historical Theology*, The Banner of Truth Trust, London, 1960, Vol II, p.333). Furthermore, the organic connection between the saved and the unsaved is itself a matter of grace. Far from being something that belongs to the very nature of things it is temporary and provisional. In the final order the sheep and the goats will be radically separated.

CHAPTER FIFTEEN

THE LIMITATIONS OF COMMON GRACE

We cannot, then, accept the arguments alleged by Hoeksema and others against the doctrine of common grace. But the limitations of common grace must be borne in mind. Otherwise we shall look at the field of human endeavour with a quite unbiblical optimism.

Theology

These limitations appear, first of all, in the practice of theology itself. The natural man can attain to a very high competence in theological knowledge. He can formally understand the doctrines, no matter how profound and mysterious. He can accurately represent the biblical teaching on the most personal aspects of religious experience. He can state, clearly and lucidly, the great principles of the Christian ethic. He can also show considerable zeal in asserting and defending these truths. And he can even derive inestimable pleasure and stimulus from the theological studies in which he is engaged. None of this goes beyond what Paul recognises in 1 Corinthians 13: 2: a man may understand all mysteries and all knowledge, even although he lacks the love which is the hallmark of real spiritual life.

Yet the dangers should not be minimised. The greatest danger for the individual is that his interest in theology may remain purely academic and the satisfaction he receives from it merely intellectual. The peril is enhanced by the fact that theology involves exposure to such a variety of disciplines: history, literature, philosophy, linguistics, psychology, natural science, and many others. The mental exhilaration derived from these can easily become a substitute for delighting in God; and because God and theology are so closely related, the pleasure we derive from the latter can all too easily blind us to our own spiritual bankruptcy. A man may see theological propositions very clearly while yet remaining completely blind to the beauty of God. He may have an intelligent and loyal commitment to a creed and yet never have committed himself to Christ nor his life to God's rule. No man is more exposed than the theologian to the risk of having the faith of devils: the belief that is intellectually clear and certain, yet morally and spiritually unproductive.

But unregenerate theology is an even greater danger to the church than it is to the individual. One might even say that the supreme tragedy of the church during the last hundred years has been that she has habitually entrusted theological education to men with no higher qualifications than those of common grace. Those qualifications have often, within the limits of their kind, been splendid: great learning and critical acumen, consummate literary and debating skill and immense personal charm. But none of this can cancel the fact that to lack special, redemptive grace - to be unregenerate - is a fatal defect in a theologian. His whole relationship with God is wrong. He lacks rapport with Him. He has never seen Him. He does not know Him. He does not recognise His voice. He is neither awed nor enthralled, neither fascinated nor intimidated. He presumes to stand over the revelation of the Almighty in pure academic detachment.

Similarly, his relationship with the church is wrong. According to E.L. Mascall, theology is an activity 'consciously operating within the worshipping and redemptive community which is the Body of Christ' (*Whatever Happened to the Human Mind,* SPCK, London, 1980, pp. ix). By such a criterion, the unregenerate theologian is in an impossible position. He is not redeemed. He does not worship. And he does not belong to the Body. His ministry creates an absurd situation in which the Seed of the Serpent purports to be feeding the Seed of the Woman, notwithstanding that there is a God-ordained enmity between the two.

This danger of an unregenerate theology exists within every stream of the Christian tradition, Evangelical as well as Catholic, Fundamentalist as well as Modernist. It creates at least four urgent problems for the church.

First, the application of wrong criteria. If the study of theology is remitted to men on academic considerations alone, they will apply purely academic criteria to their work. Their appeal will be, not to the community of the faithful, but to the community of scholars who will judge a theological treatise on the same terms as they judge a research thesis. A book or a theologian is no longer deemed important because he speaks the truth, but because he is erudite (hence the importance of bibliography), up-to-date, original, innovative, courageous and controversial. This is why historians of the theology of the last two centuries focus almost exclusively on the achievements of a succession of men from Schleiermacher to Bultmann who by the standards of historic Christianity were heretics. (See for example, A.I.C. Heron: *A Century of Protestant Theology*, Lutterworth Press, London, 1980.) The ascendancy of academic criteria is now such that no one dreams of asking whether any man's teaching is wholesome or hygienic (1 Timothy 1: 10) for the church. The judgment of the church does not matter.

The second danger presented by an unregenerate theology is that it exercises its skills from the wrong motives. Theology exists for the sake of the church. Too often, however, its modern practitioners seek only personal distinction or academic preferment, pursuing their studies with scant recollection of the body they are called to serve. They do not see themselves as the servants of the church. They do not show pastoral concern, making their publications intelligible to ordinary believers, answering their questions, resolving their doubts, strengthening their faith and in general comforting and inspiring them. They do not even try to ensure that the students under their care will be faithful and profound preachers of the gospel. Nor do they have any evangelistic concern to relate the good news of Christ to a world that lacks God and lacks hope. In fact, a good deal of contemporary theology is useless, amounting to little more than an esoteric game in which academic theologians answer questions which could occur only to academic theologians, engage in arid debate with sterile philosophies and walk up innumerable blind alleys constructed by university examination boards. To an alarming degree it meets only needs which it creates. More boldly, its only use is as its own antidote.

The third danger is that an unregenerate theology, no matter how richly endowed by common grace, will distort, suppress and even attack Christian truth. We bear in mind that this is only a danger and that a theology is not necessarily erroneous because it is the work of an unregenerate mind. As we have already seen, common grace, especially in favoured spiritual environments, can preserve from error and enable anyone who is intellectually competent to understand biblical teaching and express it accurately. Nor should we overlook the fact that regenerateness is not by itself sufficient to keep us from going astray. The theology of the born-again remains a sinful theology, seeing, at best, only as through a glass, darkly (1 Corinthians 13: 12). Yet it hardly needs argument that the risk of distortion is seriously increased when theology is practised with no real spiritual resources. The natural man is hampered by a blindness that cannot see and an enmity that refuses to be subject to the authority of revelation. The effects of these are clearly seen even in connection with general revelation. Unregenerate men hold down the truth in unrighteousness and exchange it for a lie (Romans 1: 25). The closer we come to the redemptive core of revelation the greater the danger. Christ crucified is a stumbling block to ordinary religiosity and foolishness to ordinary intelligence. Consequently, unregenerate theology can never feel comfortable in the presence of the supernaturalness, the dogmatic exclusiveness and the academic offensiveness of such doctrines as the virgin birth, the resurrection and the vicarious suffering of Christ. It will feel even less comfortable before the insistence: 'You must be born again'.

The fourth danger is probably the one we are least conscious of: the danger that our theology will be loveless. At one level this means that its burden will not be lightened by love for God nor motivated by love for our neighbour. At another, it means that we treat opponents unlovingly. The *odium theologicum* is proverbial, however varied its manifestations (from misquoting those with whom we differ to burning them at the stake). At the moment, through common grace, the conventions of academic discussion have eliminated the worst abuses of the past. But courtesy is one thing: love (*agape*) is another — to be long-suffering, to be kind, to be caring, to be self-denying. The propriety of such standards all will acknowledge. But one can conform to them only through the indwelling of the God who Himself is love.

The question of the effect of unregenerateness on Christian theology is one to which the church has given curiously little attention. It has certainly not influenced the way she has appointed her teachers. By any reasonable standard, such a lack of caution, no matter how commonplace, is absurd: especially when one remembers that the heaviest artillery turned on the faith during the last two hundred years has been that of her own army of doctors and professors.

Ethics

The second area where it is important to indicate the limitations of common grace is ethics. There are two specific dangers.

The first is an over-reliance on conscience as the arbiter of right and wrong. By common grace men have the divine law written on their hearts and their awareness of what they do is accompanied by another parallel awareness that their conduct is either praiseworthy or blameworthy (Romans 2: 15). The force of these two facts is often such that men do by nature the things contained in the law. Furthermore, the voice of conscience is not silenced even by the deepest moral degradation: even in the abyss of decadence, men know that those who do such things are worthy of death (Romans 1: 32). 'It is to be observed,' wrote Calvin, 'that though men struggle with their own convictions, and would fain not only banish God from their minds, but from heaven also, their stupefaction is never so complete as to secure them from being occasionally dragged before the divine tribunal' (*Institutes*, I. IV, 2).

None of this should blind us, however, to the fact that conscience is fallen and is no safe guide in matters of moral choice. Sometimes, the light in a man is darkness: 'those that kill you will think they are serving God' (John 16: 2). Incalculable evil has been perpetrated in the name of conscience — from Marcus Aurelius' persecution of Christians through Calvin's implication in the burning of Servetus and Cotton Mather's in the burning of witches to Episcopalian harassment of Presbyterians and the formation of para-military organisations in twentieth-century Ulster.

We face the paradoxical situation that it is always our duty to obey our consciences, while knowing that those consciences are frequently wrong. The only course open to us is to take constant pains to ensure that our moral sense is informed and sharpened by the light of Scripture and the example of Christ. Conscience is not autonomous. Whatever freedom it might claim in the face of human interference, God is its Lord and His Word binds it even on matters on which it itself has no scruples.

The second limitation derives from the first: the moral consensus which prevails in any particular community is not a sufficient guide to behaviour. This consensus is a fruit of common grace and reflects the collective conscience of society. It strengthens social cohesion and often imposes powerful restraints on individual behaviour. In too many instances, however, it is the only rule of conduct which people acknowledge, so that the right becomes merely the conventional and the good becomes the customary. The social consensus is far too variable to serve as a norm. One society condemns slavery. Another condones it. In the one, adultery is only mildly disreputable. In another it is a capital offence. The marketing techniques and commercial practices of one civilisation would be anathema in another. Common grace does not prevent these variations. Nor can it ever secure exact conformity between the *mores* of society and the categorical imperatives of revelation.

Science

The limitations of common grace are equally important in the realm of science and have, indeed, led some Christian thinkers to distinguish radically between regenerate and unregenerate science, virtually proscribing the latter and invoking the fact of its unregenerateness to justify rejection of its conclusions, especially in connection with the theory of evolution.

The influence of the regenerate/unregenerate distinction varies enormously, however, from situation to situation. As Abraham Kuyper points out, there is a very broad realm of investigation in which the difference between the two groups exerts no influence, because *palingenesis* works no change in the senses, nor in the plastic conception of visible things. In matters of mere observation and measurement, for example, the influence of regeneration is virtually nil. 'Whether a thing weighs two milligrams or three can be absolutely ascertained by everyone who can weigh' (*Encyclopedia of Sacred Theology*, London, 1899, p. 157). The same is true in matters of straightforward logical deduction since the process of formal thought is not affected by sin. There is one human logic, not two. The problems increase when *inferences* have to be made, especially if these inferences involve social, moral and religious judgements, as they do in history, psychology and sociology. They are most acute in areas of conflict between science and revelation, such as anthropology, geology and biology, where there is a grave risk of suppression and distortion under the influence of *a priori* religious and philosophical considerations.

This does not mean, however, that we can simply proscribe science; or that it is a sufficient critique of any theory to say that it is the product of unregenerate intellects. For one thing, there has been a significant overlap, historically, between the influence of the two factors. The early, Baconian impetus behind modern science was largely Christian. It was based upon Christian assumptions, applied by Christian pioneers and governed by Christian motives. This methodological foundation is still largely influential. Furthermore, the difference between the two groups — the regenerate and the unregenerate — is not absolute. If common grace enables unregenerate men to 'see clearly' in the realm of natural theology (Romans 1: 20) how much more in the realm of natural science? Again, some of the unregenerate are 'not far from the kingdom of God' (Mark 12: 34); and others will be embraced within Paul's recognition that even among the pagans there were those concerned with truth, honour, righteousness, purity and virtue (Philippians 4: 8). On the other hand, there is sin in the regenerate and a Christian can even say, 'In me, that is, in my flesh, there dwells no good thing'. Not only is the observation of the Christian scientist often inadequate and his reasoning defective, but he has his own social, political, economic and religious prejudices. All these will inevitably lead to distortion, misrepresentation and suppression in various degrees. For proof of this, we need look no further than the fact that even among the regenerate themselves there are serious divisions of opinion on virtually every question investigated by science. It is also noteworthy that Scripture itself does not write off the cognitive and intellectual competence of the natural man. It does, of course, emphasise his *spiritual* incompetence. In this sphere he is blind and even structurally deficient — he possesses no faculty of spiritual discernment (1 Corinthians 2: 14). But this sweeping judgment is limited to the things of the Spirit. In other respects the children of this world may be wiser than the children of light (Luke 16: 8). The skills basic to civilisation (tent-making, cattle-herding, music building and metal-work) are depicted by Scripture as first emerging among the Cainites, not the Sethites (Genesis 4: 16-24). The art of writing and the use of papyrus are pagan skills, later baptised into Christ. The architectural and building skills of the heathen ('there is not among us any that can hew timber like the Sidonians', 1 Kings 5: 6) were as essential to the building of the temple as the skills of Bezaleel and Aholiab had been earlier to the erection of the tabernacle. Paul even endorses some of the sentiments of the heathen poets: 'As certain also of your own poets have said, "For we are also his offspring"' (Acts 17: 28).

What then should be our attitude to the current scientific consensus granting that, to a significant degree, it has been moulded by unregenerate men?

First, gratitude. Paul's assurance that 'all things' belong to the church cannot exclude the findings of pure science and the technology which flows from them. The creation mandate to subdue and colonise the earth is being fulfilled by the race organically — an amalgam of regenerate and unregenerate men from which we can escape only by 'going out of the world'. The scientific achievements of natural men are to be welcomed as cordially as their political, literary and philosophical contributions.

Secondly, repentance for the folly of some of the church's reactions to science in the past. Not only Roman Catholics but Protestants of the eminence of John Owen were guilty of condemning Galileo; and many nineteenth century clergymen blundered with little preparation into the debate on cosmogony and geology. Today, we seem to be little wiser and appear determined to make fools of ourselves in a wide variety of fields ranging from the textual criticism of the New Testament to genetics, brain science and heart-transplants.

But then, thirdly, caution. The presence of sin means that there is always the possibility of distortion and misrepresentation. The obligation to give a courteous hearing always stands, even if sometimes only on the basis of loving our enemies. But so does the presumption of imperfection and the need to subject every thesis to careful analysis and, if necessary, thorough refutation. The mere fact that the thesis is a product of unregenerate men is not in itself a refutation. But it does alert us to the possibility that subjective and personal factors may lead to false perspectives, inaccurate observation and defective logic. The closer we come to matters of theological and spiritual concern, the greater the danger.

Art

Reformed theology fully recognised art as a divine gift sustained by common grace. While acknowledging that 'the liberal arts and sciences have descended to us from the heathen', Calvin nevertheless declares: 'The invention of arts and of other things which serve to the common use and convenience of life, is a gift of God by no means to be despised' (*Commentary on Genesis,* 4: 20).

Reservations were expressed, however, in two specific areas.

First, the matter of pictorial representations of the deity. The Old Testament emphatically forbade any images of God — not only images of pagan deities but images of the true God as well (Exodus 20: 4). Calvin and his successors accepted this unquestioningly: 'His glory is defiled and His truth corrupted by the lie whenever He is set before our eyes in a visible form. God is insulted, not only when His worship is transferred to idols, but when we try to represent Him by any outward similitude' (*Harmony of the Pentateuch, ad* Exodus 20: 4). The question of images of Jesus is more difficult. For Calvin, it was enough that He was a divine person. We cannot, however, overlook the fact that Christ took human nature. The argument of the Old Testament when prohibiting images is precisely that 'you saw no manner of similitude on the day that the Lord spoke unto you in Horeb out of the midst of the fire' (Deuteronomy 4: 15). This argument cannot be applied to Christ because He was 'made in the likeness of men and found in appearance as a man' (Philippians 2: 7, 8). It is not, then, misleading or blasphemous to depict Him in a human form or to endeavour, however unsuccessfully, to represent pictorially the events described in the gospels. The danger remains, however, that the art will become bad theology, as in the case of Holman Hunt's *The Light of the World,* which depicts Christ standing impotent at the door of the human heart frustrated by the fact that the latch is on the inside.

The other reservation related to drama. The problem was not the art-form itself but the moral effect on actors and actresses. 'Too often,' wrote Abraham Kuyper, 'the prosperity of theatres is purchased at the cost of manly character and of female purity. And the purchase of delight for the ear and the eye at the price of such a moral hecatomb, the Calvinist, who honoured whatever was human in man for the sake of God, could not but condemn' (*Lectures on Calvinism*, p. 75). A society which idolises the stars of show-business may find such sentiments difficult to comprehend. But Kuyper's assessment is little different from that of Desmond Morris, who, having spoken of prostitution, goes on to say: 'A milder form of sex-for-material-gain is executed by strip-teasers, dance hostesses, beauty queens, club-girls, dancers, models and many *actresses*. For payment, they provide ritualised performances of the earlier stages of the sexual sequence, but stop short of copulation itself' (*The Human Zoo*, London, 1971, p. 100). In his fears as to the effects of theatre on manliness of character, Kuyper is following closely in the footsteps of Plato who, although not banning the theatre altogether, forbade his philosopher-rulers to be character actors: 'The only characters on which they must model themselves must be men of courage, self-control, independence and religious principle. They must no more act a mean part than do a mean action or any other kind of wrong. For we soon reap the fruits of literature in life, and prolonged indulgence in any form of literature leaves its mark on the moral nature of man' (*The Republic*, Penguin Edition, 1959, p. 134). In accordance with this outlook, the future Guardians could not play the roles of women, slaves, madmen, cowards, rogues or manual workers: which means much the same as saying they could not act at all. Whether Plato was correct in claiming that people become the roles they play is obviously debateable. For the moment, we need only observe that when Abraham Kuyper expressed some reservations about the theatre he was not making a totally eccentric point peculiar to Calvinism. Spokesmen of other cultures, ranging from the classical meritocracy to the modern permissive society, have said the same thing.

It would be precipitate to conclude that drama in itself is wrong. The genius of Shakespeare and Ibsen, Olivier and Glenda Jackson, are gifts of common grace. The problem lies in the prevailing public demand (much older than the twentieth century) for the sleazy and the suggestive, and the all too obvious willingness of actors, playwrights and theatre managers to accommodate it.

Common grace provides us with a biblical rationale for involvement in the world. But that involvement must never become incautious or unthinking. Human society lies in the Evil One (1 John 5: 19), and a balanced Christian statement must embrace not only world-affirmation but also, and equally, world-renunciation and denial.

CHAPTER SIXTEEN

LOVE DIVINE, ALL LOVES EXCELLING

The love of God is sometimes discussed as a mere sub-division of His goodness (*Shorter Catechism*, Ans. 4). But this hardly does justice to its importance in biblical revelation. God *is* love (1 John 4: 8), as He is spirit (John 4: 24), light (1 John 1: 5) and a consuming fire (Hebrews 12: 29). Love is His innermost nature. He not simply has love or exercises love. It is His very form that He looks on the things of others (Philippians 2: 4f.) and it is in this above all that He stands forth not as an abstraction but as a person, confronting others in the offer of fellowship (1 John 1: 3).

Moreover, nothing bears more closely upon our plight than the revelation of God's love. We are tiny, lonely specks on the face of an almost infinite universe, quantitatively insignificant, involved in a sequence of events in which all is vanity, and constantly threatened, individually and collectively, by the march of history. Yet into this sense of insecurity and lack of identity there shines the love of God. We matter: we matter immensely. That is what lightens our darkness, what redeems our lives from the threat of meaninglessness and causes our hearts to make melody always and in all things.

In agreement with this, the New Testament constantly sees the love of God as the supreme message of Calvary, itself the most stupendous utterance of God. The giving of the only-begotten so that the world should have eternal life (John 3: 16) — the dying of Christ for us while we were still enemies (Romans 5: 10) — the giving of the Son as the propitiation for our sins (1 John 4: 10): what these declare above all is the love of God! And what is God's most stupendous word is also the supreme object of our human enquiry: 'that ye may be able to know the love of Christ, which passes knowledge' (Ephesians 3: 19).

It is clear from such considerations that the love of God is one of the primary emphases of Scripture. We are therefore unfaithful to the biblical vision if we treat it merely as a sub-division of some other aspect of God's character. It deserves prominence commensurate with the clarity with which it was revealed on Calvary, its special relevance to our redemption and, in its Christian form, its stupendous unexpectedness.

Biblical terms

The distinctive New Testament word for love is *agape*. There is nothing of any theological significance in its etymology or in its usage in secular Greek. In fact, its great advantage was that it was little used and therefore free from the compromising associations of the usual words for love. It was an empty, conveniently available vessel, into which Christian revelation could pour the full meaning of its own unique proclamation of love.

Three other words were in general use: *philia* (friendship-love), *storge* (family affection) and *eros* (marital or sexual love). All of these, however, had associations which might have obscured the specific message spoken on Calvary. The affection of which they all spoke was natural. It was rooted either in blood relationship or in physical attraction or in loveliness of character or in affinity of personality. *Agape* does not in and of itself mean love for the unlovely. It is used, for example, of the Father's love for the Son and the Son's love for the Father and this love presupposes, of course, the very closest affinity and the most perfect loveableness. But the New Testament proclamation cannot be contained within these bounds. God loved the world. He loved His enemies. *Philia* could not cope with that. It was for friends. Nor could *storge*. That was for the family circle and blood relations. Nor could *eros*. That presupposed beauty and attractiveness. *Agape* had no such associations and it could well express the great message of love for the sinful world — for what was hostile and ugly.

It is possible, however, to drive too large a wedge between *agape* and the other words, especially *eros*. The *agape* of God is utterly gracious and it does not depend, as *eros* does, on any loveliness in its object. But *agape* does not, in contrast with *eros*, mean a love without involvement, without commitment or — if we may dare — without passion. We must remember that the love of God for sinful man was first expressed not in Greek, but in Hebrew. The primary word used here is *ahabhah*. For example, 'In his love and in his pity he redeemed them', writes Isaiah (63: 9). ' I have loved thee with an everlasting love' says the Lord in Jeremiah (31: 3). And again, 'I drew them with cords of a man , with bands of love' (Hosea 11: 4). In all these the word used for love is *ahabhah* and, in the words of one Old

Testament theologian, 'the human experience from which the basic meaning is derived is the overwhelming force of passion between men and women' (Eichrodt, *Theology of the Old Testament*, Vol. I, p. 250). It is enough to remember that the word is used repeatedly in the Song of Solomon (e.g. 2: 4, 2: 5, 2: 7).

Confirmation of the fact that the divine *agape* must retain some of the nuances of *eros* is found in Hosea's portrayal of the relation between Jehovah and Israel as a marriage: 'And it shall be at that day, saith the Lord, that thou shalt call me, My husband. And I will betroth thee unto me for ever; yea I will betroth thee unto me in faithfulness and thou shalt know the Lord' (Hosea 2: 16, 19, 20). This is continued into the New Testament where both Paul and John speak very expressly of the church as the bride of Christ (Ephesians 5: 22-33, Revelation 19: 7, 21: 9, 22: 17). These facts cannot be ignored in any attempt to understand *agape* as an expression of God's attitude to the world. Clearly it lacks any erotic emphasis (although the Old Testament, especially Hosea, living in the midst of Baalite fertility-cults, took the risk of being misunderstood at this point). It also breaks through the normal understanding of *eros* as love for one who is at least *considered attractive*.

The world that God loved was in the wicked one. Indeed the unworthiness of the beloved Israel is so vividly described by Ezekiel that we feel a rising feeling of disgust as we see what it was that God betrothed to Himself: 'In the day that thou wast born thy navel was not cut, neither wast thou washed in water to supple thee; thou wast not salted at all, nor swaddled at all; but thou wast cast out in the open field to the loathing of thy person in the day that thou wast born! And when I passed by thee, and saw thee polluted in thine own blood, I said unto thee when thou wast in thy blood, *live*' (Ezekiel 16: 4-6). But *agape* is still *eros* to the extent that God's love is deep and passionate, extravagant, fully committed, possessive and jealous. It is absolutely in earnest. God is determined to have the church's fellowship, to redeem His bride and to present Her to Himself holy and without blemish (Ephesians 5: 27). He is grieved by apostasy as a husband is grieved by the faithlessness of his wife; and He nourishes and cherishes His church more extravagantly than the most doting husband.

Conversely, the attitude of the church to Him, when the church is what it should be, is also one of profound longing and passionate commitment. 'There is none on earth that I desire besides thee,' says the Psalmist (73: 25). He pants for the living God (42: 1) and his flesh longs for Him in a dry and thirsty land (63: 1). Paul is only expressing the same sentiment when he writes, 'For me to live is Christ' (Philippians 1: 21). These longings on the part of believers do not go beyond God's interest in them and His commitment to them. They only reciprocate His love.

The Supreme Elucidation of Love

The supreme elucidation of *agape*, however, is the divine self-giving on Calvary: 'God so loved the world that he gave his only begotten Son that whosoever believes in him should not perish but should have everlasting life' (John 3: 16). The fact that God's love is an utterly gracious commitment to the totally unworthy is clearly highlighted. It is for the *world.* The world here, as often in the thought of John, is less a quantitative than a qualitative concept. The emphasis is not so much on the universalness of God's love as on the *worldliness* of the constituency which God loves. The world lies in the evil one; it hates Christ and the church; it is something from which believers must keep themselves unspotted, to which they must not conform, from which they must separate and which they must overcome. From one point of view Christians are explicitly forbidden to love it. 'The world,' concludes B.B. Warfield, 'is just the synonym for all that is evil and noisome and disgusting. There is nothing in it that can attract God's love, nay, that can justify the love of any good man. It is a thing not to be dallied with, or acquiesced in' (*Biblical and Theological Studies*, Presbyterian and Reformed, Philadelphia, 1952, p. 514). Yet God loved it, dominated as it was by the flesh and the devil, composed of those who were enmity against God, and organised specifically in opposition to His will. This at last is our encouragement — God's love condescends to reach and embrace us in the very depth of our degradation, even at the point (Calvary) where human hatred against Him burns most clearly, where the defiance is most explicit and the loathsomeness most evident.

But Calvary also underlines the fact that the divine *agape* will not rest until it has bestowed upon us the very highest benefits. This love is in order to our having 'eternal life'. It is not niggardly. It is immeasurable, even extravagant. The blessing of God is as plentiful as the dew upon Mount Hermon (Psalm

133: 3). *Agape*, in its full expression, confers upon us every spiritual blessing (Ephesians 1: 3). It undertakes that all things shall work together for our good, that only goodness and mercy shall follow us all the days of our lives and that we shall dwell in the house of the Lord for ever. Above all, it gives us a share in God's love for His own Son. Christ prays, 'That the love wherewith thou hast loved me may be in them and I in them' (John 17: 26). On the face of it, it is incredible that the Father should love us with the very love which He has for His Son. Yet this is the plain meaning of this kind of passage. It is true that we may distinguish between the status of the Son as the Eternal Word and the status of the Son as Mediator. In the last analysis, however, the Eternal Word and the Mediator are one and the same being. God's love for the Eternal Word embraces the Mediator; and in embracing the Mediator it encloses every member of His body, all His friends, all His brethren and each single one of His sheep. We are elect in Christ. In Him we have the adoption. The manner of God's love for us is that we, with Him, should be called the sons of God. The language is at last utterly unambiguous and explicit. We are joint-heirs with Christ (Romans 8:17). We have the same inheritance. And when we ask what the inheritance is we receive the staggering answer that we are heirs of God. He is Christ's inheritance. He is ours. He is for us. Nothing could be more extravagant than that. We are part of the fellowship of the Father and His Son, Jesus Christ (1 John 1: 3) and, consequently, Paul can pray, in respect of every Christian, that we might be filled with all the fullness of God (Ephesians 3: 19). That very fullness (*pleroma)* which is the glory and the form of Christ — we are to be filled with that.

The other point with regard to the divine *agape* which is emphasized on Calvary is that it spares no cost. God gave His only begotten Son. The same point is made more fully in Romans 8: 32, which declares that God 'did not spare His own Son but delivered Him up for us all'. What is in view in these passages is a priestly act on the part of God the Father in which He offers His Son for the sin of the world. It is a complex act. He gives Him to be the church's Head and the world's Saviour. He prepares for Him a body in which our sins might be borne (1 Peter 2: 24). He sends Him into the world (Galatians 4: 4). He delivers Him up to Judas, to the Jews and to Pilate. But the process does not end there. Behind all the horrendousness of Calvary there is the agency of God. He lays on His Son the iniquity of us all (Isaiah 53: 6). He bruises Him and makes His soul an offering for sin (Isaiah 53: 10). He made Him sin (2 Corinthians 5: 21). He condemns sin in the flesh of His own Son (Romans 8: 3). He does not spare Him, allowing neither the uniqueness of His status nor the promptings of His own love to modify the condemnation or to mitigate the pain. He is given over unreservedly to all that sin deserved.

The meaning of God's love can only be understood as we see that the *giving* involved the imputation of our sin to Christ and His enduring of all that it meant to answer for that sin before God. We must never lose sight, however, of the complementary and paradoxical fact that the Son is never other than an object of the Father's love. He is never disowned or despised. He is never hated. He is always 'My beloved Son, in whom I am well pleased'. He is sent into the low condition of our humanness as the Loved One. Indeed, this is the glory of the Father's love for the world. Its interests — our interests— take precedence, for a moment, over those of the Son, although it is also part of God's great purpose that His love for His Son will express itself in highly exalting Him as a reward for His obedience. It is important to remember the cost to the Father arising out of His love for His Son. How Abraham felt as he brought to the altar his son, his only son, Isaac whom he loved; how David felt as he cried, 'Absalom, my son, my son! Would I had died for thee Absalom, my son, my son!' — These are but shadows of the cost to God, as the love of these fathers for their sons was but a faint reflection of God's love for His. We lose much if our doctrine of the impassibility of God obscures from us the implications of the depth of the Father's affection. When God contemplated the possibility of chastising Israel He did so with the profoundest anguish: 'How shall I give thee up? My heart is turned within me, my repentings are kindled together. I will not execute the fierceness of mine anger, I will not return to destroy Ephraim' (Hosea 11: 8-9). With what hesitation and misgivings and reluctance and sorrow did such a God — who does not at any time afflict willingly and for whom judgment is a strange work — with what reluctance does He bruise His Son and awake His sword against His very fellow!

But why in any case does God's love for the world find expression at such appalling cost to His Son? Here indeed we see only through a glass darkly and very soon reach the limits of revelation. But two points may be made.

First, the Son stands in the judgment-hall *voluntarily*. He came into the world. He sets His face steadfastly towards Calvary. He loved the church and gave Himself for it. He is in the anathema only because, having loved His own who were in the world, He loved them to the end (John 13: 1). Undoubtedly, He endures the judgment in unmitigated fullness. But He does so not only of His own volition, but eagerly. He is 'straitened until it be accomplished' (Luke 12: 50). In the adoring words of 'Rabbi' Duncan: 'It was damnation, and He took it lovingly!' He loves the world so much that He identifies with it completely. He becomes men's representative, prepared to act for them, sharing the whole entail of their sin. But more! He becomes their substitute, not only suffering along with them but suffering instead of them, and suffering with such effect that what He suffered His church will never suffer. They will never know the depths out of which He cried, 'My God, my God, why hast thou forsaken me?' (Mark 15: 34).

The second point to be made here is that the Father and the Son are at last one. The unity of God is as fundamental to Christian as to Jewish thought: 'Hear, O Israel: Jehovah your God is one Jehovah' (Deuteronomy 6: 4). The implications of this for the doctrine of the atonement are far-reaching. The judge and the victim are not two different beings. Jesus and the Father are one (John 10: 30), just as the Lord is the Spirit (2 Corinthians 3: 17). On Calvary, Jehovah condemns sin. He curses it. He puts it outside (Hebrews 13: 12). Equally, however, He bears it. He imputes it to Himself. He receives its wages. He becomes Himself its propitiation. He becomes the sinner's ransom. He becomes even the sinner's advocate — God with God. Certainly, we must not ignore or obscure the distinction between God the Father and God the Son. Equally, however, we must avoid the more prevalent danger of regarding the Father and the Son as different beings. In the last analysis, God expresses His love for us not by putting another to suffer in our place but by Himself taking our place. He meets the whole cost of our forgiveness in Himself by exacting it of Himself. He demands the ransom. He provides the ransom. He becomes the ransom. Herein is love.

Whom does it embrace?

The biblical teaching on the love of God confronts the Calvinist with a question of real urgency: What is the extent of God's love? Whom does it embrace? And is it at all possible, against the background of predestination, to speak of God loving all men?

At the most basic level this love finds expression within the triune life of God Himself. We are walking near the edge of well-nigh blasphemous speculation if, with Hoeksema, we interpret this as meaning that love is the expression of God's absolute and pure self-centredness (*Reformed Dogmatics*, p. 103). God is love, eternally and quite independently of creation. But His eternal love was not introverted, narcissistic and self-regarding. It was a love expressed in the fellowship of the eternal Trinity. In the beginning, there was not only God, but God with God: 'the Word was with God'. Indeed, if we may translate literally, 'the Word was *towards* God'. There was an outgoing in affection and glory between the Father and the Son and between the Son and the Spirit. The Father and the Son are not so distinct that they are two separate beings. But they are so distinct that the one is the object of the other's love. To each, the other is the beloved.

This eternal love embraces equally the Son after His incarnation. He comes, by enfleshment, into creaturehood, dependence, frailty, poverty, wretchedness and degradation. But His identity remains the same as before. The child in the manger is the Lord of all. In Gethsemane (and no less on Calvary) He is still the Son, and more than once — as at the baptism and the transfiguration — He is reminded of that. God comforts Him by flooding His consciousness with the assurance that He is uniquely beloved. Consequently, at every point in His service He is splendidly upheld (Isaiah 42: 1) and at its close He is highly exalted — raised as high as the overflowing love of God can contrive.

The Son fully reciprocates the Father's love. He delights to do His will and to finish the work given to Him. The separation involved in His coming into the world is immeasurably painful and the prospect of returning to the Father fills Him with delight (John 14: 28). All the glory He seeks is to be 'with the Father'; and at last, when every enemy has been subdued and every son of God has been brought home, He gladly surrenders the kingdom to the Father, so that He may still be all in all (1 Corinthians 15: 28).

God's love for the world

But love is also God's attitude to the world. There must be no hesitation. The world is ugly and unlovely and some of its constituents will be finally and irrevocably lost. Yet we cannot stop short of saying that God loves it. This is made splendidly clear in the words of our Lord recorded in Matthew 5: 43-48. We are to be perfect as our Father in heaven is perfect; and it is part of that perfection that we are to love our enemies. Indeed, that is the very glory of the Father's perfection. He makes His sun rise on the evil as well as on the good and sends rain on the just equally with the unjust. To love our enemies is to emulate God — a fact which clearly implies that His love extends to those who are not yet reconciled to Him and even to those who are *never* reconciled.

The first element in this love of God for the world is His long-suffering. He exercises such forbearance that all men must confess, 'With us He dealt not as we sinned'.

Secondly, as the passage already quoted from Matthew shows, God's attitude to the world is one of benevolence. Even to those who refuse to acknowledge Him, there flows an unceasing stream of good and perfect gifts — sun, rain, fruitful seasons, food, gladness and all the domestic, social, cultural and technological consequences of common grace. We should note, in passing, that this benevolence is not haphazard and unpredictable. It is covenantal, in terms of God's covenant with all mankind in Noah: 'While the earth remaineth, seedtime and harvest, and cold and heat, and summer and winter, and day and night shall not cease' (Genesis 8:22).

Thirdly, and most important, God's love for the world means that He will have all men to be saved (1 Timothy 2:4). This is not to say that God has decreed the salvation of every human being — a doctrine which would lead to universalism and carry us far beyond the position of classical Arminianism. But God will have all men to be saved in the sense that He has provided a salvation suited to the needs of all. The blood of Christ 'makes the vilest clean'. Furthermore, the salvation is offered to all. The church must preach the good news to every creature (Mark 16: 15) and, as the ambassador of Christ, plead with all those, without exception, who are exposed to the terror of the Lord (2 Corinthians 5: 20). Scripture makes clear that this total openness of the gospel-call expresses the very heart of God's own attitude to the world. He has no pleasure in the death of the wicked, but longs that they should turn and live (Ezekiel 33: 11). This is why He pleads, 'Turn ye! turn ye! why will ye die?' And this is why, in the flesh, as He beholds the city, He weeps over it, stirred by the thought of its lostness and its imminent ruin (Luke 19:41). 'How often,' He says elsewhere, 'would I have gathered thy children together as a hen gathers her chickens under her wings!' And how firmly is the responsibility placed where it belongs: '*You* would not, you were not willing!' (Matthew 23: 37).

The Christian evangelist, then, has good news for every creature. God is love. Christ has suffered for sins once and for all. Redemption is offered freely to every man. How seriously and cordially this was accepted in Reformed theology appears very clearly in *The Marrow of Modern Divinity*, beloved by Thomas Boston and his spiritual successors in Scotland. According to *The Marrow* we are to answer the question, 'What must I do to be saved?' by saying: 'Be verily persuaded in your heart that Jesus Christ is yours, and that you shall have life and salvation by Him; that whatsoever Christ did for the redemption of mankind, He did it for you' (*The Marrow of Modern Divinity* with notes by the Rev. Thomas Boston, Edinburgh, 1818, p. 144). To the same effect are the following words from Preston's *Treatise on Faith*: 'Go and tell every man without exception that there is good news for him, Christ is dead for him; and if he will take Him and accept of His righteousness, he shall have Him' (cited in *The Marrow*, p. 148).

As Boston is careful to point out, however, this does not mean that we have by nature and simply as sinners a 'saving interest' in Christ. He is not ours in the sense that we are already saved. He is not ours by possession. But He is ours 'in the deed of gift and grant to mankind lost'. Even before we believe, Christ is ours in the sense of being freely offered to us in the gospel. He is not ours in the sense that we already possess Him, but He is ours in the sense that we have, simply as sinners, an immediate right to move in and take possession of Him (*The Marrow*, as cited, p. 144).

But may we also say, 'Christ is dead for you'? This phraseology is obviously undesirable from a Christological point of view. Christ is not dead. The point being made, however, is that Christ, who died for sinners and who now stands in the midst of the throne as one who has been slain, offers Himself and all the benefits secured by His death to every sinner. He is there as one who died for sinners and who is available for all men to come to. It means, says Boston, 'Tell every man, "A Saviour is provided for him; that is, for him to come to and believe on: there is a crucified Christ for him, the ordinance of heaven for salvation for lost man, in making use of which he may be saved"' (*op. cit.*, p. 158).

It is clear, then, that the love of God for all men as expressed in the free offer of Christ and His salvation is something which Reformed theology has been at pains to conserve and even to emphasize. But Boston's distinction between Christ being *offered* and Christ being *possessed* is crucially important. The same distinction, with a slight change in terminology, is found in another great Scottish theologian, Stewart of Cromarty, who wrote: 'Beware of confounding promises and invitations — two very distinct things and addressed to two different classes. The invitations are to sinners; the promises to saints only' (*The Tree of Promise*, Edinburgh, 1866, p. LV). This is not to make grace conditional, but it is to remind ourselves that not all to whom God's love and salvation are offered are actually saved. There is an indispensable human response to the offer of the gospel. God *requires* of us repentance, faith and a diligent use of the outward means of grace (*Shorter Catechism* 85). The offer of salvation is made to all men — to the unbelieving and impenitent. But the actual promise of salvation is confined to the believing. This is made very plain in John 3: 16, where both the universalism of the offer and the particularism of the promise are equally emphasized. The world is loved. But only those who believe in Christ have eternal life. Even the elect, until they come to Christ, are children of wrath (Ephesians 2: 3).

It follows from this that the whole concern of Christian evangelism must be to elicit the response that God commands. The good news is not that all men *are* saved, but that if they come to Christ they *will be* saved. Every man — sinner, ungodly, unbelieving, impenitent, hypocrite, backslider — is to be invited and even pleaded with. But only those who receive Christ Jesus as Lord are to be given the comfort, 'Your sins are forgiven'. To evoke that response we may tell them that Christ loves them so much that He offers to be their Saviour and pleads with them to accept Him. But they must *come*. If the offering love is spurned — if the crucified Christ is rejected — they are lost. Indeed, the very gravity of unbelief in the face of evangelism is precisely that it is a rejection of so great a love and so great a Saviour.

Love for the elect

The third constituency embraced by the love of God is the elect. This love is distinguished by the fact that it is specifically

God's determination to conform them to the image of His own Son (Romans 8: 29). He so loves them that He has prepared a kingdom for them and has undertaken to do all in His power to bring them to that destiny. His electing love is a total, unqualified commitment to His own people. In their case He does not only send out the invitations and plead with them. He is not content merely to weep over them. He creates in them the response which He commands, opening their hearts and uniting them to Christ.

Such a conception of the love of God is unique to Calvinism. Arminianism believes that God so loves all men that He has made their salvation possible, if only they believe. It also believes that God so loves all men that He offers them this salvation freely. The Calvinist believes all that and the Arminian believes nothing more. But the Calvinist believes, in addition, that God loves some men — not a tiny, pathetic clique, but a multitude which no man can number, drawn from every race, language, colour and culture — with a unique and special love. He has not only made their salvation possible and freely available. He applies it to each of them and cares for them, meticulously and sedulously, until they are completely Christ-like. He specifically and actually saves them.

Electing, redemptive love is utterly realistic. God *knows* those He loves. Indeed, in many passages of Scripture *to know* is virtually synonymous with *to love*. God's love is totally perceptive. The beloved are enemies, alien and ungodly. They are such when He loves them. He knows they are such. And yet He loves them. His love, as James Packer points out, is 'based at every point on prior knowledge of the worst about me, so that no discovery now can disillusion Him about me, in the way I am so often disillusioned about myself, and quench His determination to bless me' (*Knowing God*, Hodder and Stoughton, 1973, p. 37). The commitment is no less omniscient than loving: and it is irreversible.

It is also extravagant, bestowing its blessings with infinite largesse. He gives every spiritual blessing (Ephesians 1: 3), He ordains that all things are ours. He works all things together for our good and He bestows His Spirit without measure. As the incident of the anointing at Bethany shows, it is of the very essence of love to be careless of cost. Mary's affection can find expression only in a deed which, to the onlookers, is utterly wasteful. God's giving His Son for the world is surely in the same category. The elder brother is introduced into the parable of the Prodigal precisely to highlight the fact that love goes beyond the bounds of reason when it makes so splendid a provision for such a wastrel. God's love will not rest until it has placed His people in the very glory which Christ had with the Father before the world was. They will be hyper-conquerors (Romans 8: 37) and hyper-exalted (Philippians 2: 9).

THE END

Jesus, Divine Messiah: The Old Testament Witness

Robert L. Reymond

A scholarly expostion of eight Old Testament passages describing the work of the Messiah.

The late Robert L. Reymond was Professor of Systematic Theology and Apologetics at Covenant Theological Seminary, St Louis, U.S.A.

128 pp. ISBN 0 906731 94 1 large paperback

The
Root and Branch

Joseph A. Pipa

The book explores the mystery of Christ's two natures, leading us to know Christ better.

'A full and excellent introduction to what the Bible has to say about Christ' - Sinclair Ferguson

Dr. Pipa is pastor of Covenant Presbyterian Church, Houston, Texas

128pp. ISBN 1 871676 16 9 large paperback

The Spirit of Promise

Donald Macleod

The author encourages believers to discover what their spiritual role is in the local church and gives advice on how the Spirit guides Christians.

The author is Professor of Systematic Theology in the Free Church College, Edinburgh.

112pp *large paperback*